The **POWER** _of_
FORGIVENESS

The POWER *of* FORGIVENESS

WHY IT'S GOOD TO FORGIVE YOUR FRIEND, YOUR BOSS, YOUR FAMILY AND EVERYONE WHO HURTS AND BETRAYS

JANISE BEAUMONT

inspired LIVING

ALLEN&UNWIN

First published in 2009 by Allen & Unwin

Allen & Unwin
83 Alexander Street
Crows Nest NSW 2065
Australia
Phone: (61 2) 8425 0100
Fax: (61 2) 9906 2218
Email: info@allenandunwin.com
Web: www.allenandunwin.com

Cataloguing-in-Publication details are available
from the National Library of Australia
www.librariesaustralia.nla.gov.au

ISBN 978 1 74175 767 5

Set in 11/14 pt Minion Pro by Bookhouse, Sydney
Printed in Australia by McPherson's Printing Group

10 9 8 7 6 5 4 3 2 1

CONTENTS

1 Don't Get Mad. Get Even   1

Part One
DON'T GET MAD . . . GET EVEN

2 Queen of Mean   7
3 Payback, or Let It Go   10
4 Sometimes Forgiveness Finds *YOU*   12
5 When You Lose Everything   15
6 Victim No More   19
7 From Riding High in LA . . . to Rock Bottom   22
8 Picking Up the Pieces   27
9 Forgiveness Can't Be Faked   30
10 Is Revenge the Ultimate Orgasm?   36

Part two
MIRACLES HAPPEN

11 Miracles Happen!   41
12 Forgiving Doesn't Have to Mean You'll Be Best Buddies   43
13 We All Have Unfinished Business   46
14 Being Stuck in Non-Forgiveness   48
15 When Work is Hell   50
16 Happiness is the Best Revenge   54
17 End of the Affair   57
18 Happy Endings Against the Odds   59
19 Secret Romance in a Wardrobe   62

Part three
IT'S OFFICIAL . . .

20	It's Official: Forgiveness is Good for You	67
21	Starting Over	71
22	Wired For Bliss	74
23	Don't Leave Your Song Unsung	77
24	When Someone Wants You Dead	80
25	Fake It 'til You Make It	82
26	Don't Sweat the Small Stuff	85
27	Forgiveness Poster Boys	89
28	Great Suffering, Followed by Forgiveness	91
29	Losing at Love, and Still Coming Out a Winner	93
30	When Loves Goes Bad—Get Over It!	96

Part Four
FORGIVING YOURSELF

31	Forgiving Yourself . . . That's the Tough One	101
32	When Family Life is a Battlefield	107
33	Take a Chance: Step Outside Your Comfort Zone	117
34	Woman in a Million	119
35	Life Beyond Revenge	122
36	Conditional Forgiveness	124
37	Hurting Like Hell, But Forgiving Anyway	127
38	Joy At Last!	132
39	The Forgiveness Diet	143

DON'T GET MAD. GET EVEN

I'm guessing here, but I figure hate is a bit like heroin. Both make you feel fabulous for a time, then they start to eat at you from the inside out. Eventually, the chances of you reaching your full potential are in danger of being shot to bits. The joke is, while you continue to loathe and despise someone long after the event—say the girl or guy who beat you to a lead role in a school production of *Grease*—you're only hurting yourself, while the bitch who played Sandy, or the creep who shone as Danny, is probably enjoying life way more than you.

There's great magic in learning to forgive. So get with the program and learn to bless the friend who caused you to sob into your pillow all those years ago when you were robbed of your moment in the spotlight.

This is no easy task—not if you're someone like me, who could have easily won Gold in the Olympics if hating had been an event. I had a great mentor in hate in the early days. Amanda taught me that 'If you wait long enough, you get your moment'—meaning that the chance for revenge will come, and will be just as sweet, even if a couple of years have gone by. 'Patience is the key to karma', Amanda explained . . . and she was not advocating easing up on resentment while you put your life on hold. You weren't supposed to stop longing for that golden opportunity to arrive, to balance the books, not for a moment.

So I moved it up a notch and on to a much more spiritual plane, and my mantra became: Get even, and *then* forgive. Now I was in the zone where it's much easier to absolve a cheating boyfriend if I first sneaked into his apartment and cut the sleeves off his new Hugo Boss jacket: get busy with the scissors, *then* face the dreaded f-word.

My mantra became: Get even, and then forgive.

I've never told this to anyone, but there was a guy I dated for only a few months as eventually he began to appal me with the way he regarded women as little more than Barbies. When we broke up, I prayed his next girlfriend would dump him, as he had dumped me, and that this would be my satisfying retribution. When this did indeed happen, for a nanosecond I felt a warm glow from the news, then felt kind of empty. But as God is my witness, I never went as far as hiring a professional to break the kneecaps of any lover or boss who had wronged me, as is the way in Hollywood movies. A plan that could backfire spectacularly had no place in my schemes. I was more of a passive–aggressive payback princess.

Someone I went to school with told me once: 'Boys don't hold grudges like girls do. It's one of their great strengths.' Her comment struck me right in the gut, because it allowed me to see for the first time that forgiving and moving on is what sets us free. Boys make up, forget the whole thing, and are soon back having fun together, while girls who fall out can be hell-bent on vengeance. So I wonder, who are the smart ones here?

Part One
DON'T GET MAD
. . . GET EVEN

2

QUEEN OF MEAN

When I was working for a paper in London, I lived with a Fleet Street journalist. The relationship ran hot and cold on my side. I was the queen of mean, treating him badly on a regular basis, knowing all along that he loved me very much. I could have been kinder; I realise that now. I was then blown away with the classy way he farewelled me at the airport. As he hugged me for the last time, I admitted with regret that I had been a piece of work, often hurting him. He replied: 'But it was worth it. I'd do it all again.'

He truly wasn't angry with me, and he wasn't going to hold a grudge. I found his grace and generosity inspiring. I settled into my seat on a plane bound for New York, vowing to try to ditch the rage I carried for a stack of men and women in my past. And here's the weirdest part: as I looked out the window, watching London airport fade from view, I actually remembered several people I'd been refusing to forgive for so long that I couldn't remember what they'd done to make me hate them so much. For all I knew, it had been a misunderstanding—and yet I went on loathing them, using up all that energy for no good reason.

By the time the flight attendant handed me my second gin and tonic, I promised myself I'd try and get smart. I was crazy! I suddenly had a vision of me as a shrivelled-up old prune by forty if I didn't develop the knack of bouncing back from disappointments and doublecrosses.

Interestingly, a test came my way the next weekend. I was staying with a couple in Connecticut. Another old friend had flown in from San Francisco, so the four of us were looking forward to a fun couple of days together and things got off to a great start, but fell part in the worst way.

It all began with a silly conversation. We were attempting to outdo each other with stories about rude shop assistants in high-end boutiques (à la Julia Roberts's experience in *Pretty Woman*). Our hosts, Mike and Cindy, had hilarious anecdotes to share, then it was my turn: 'You all remember Dan who I used to go out with? Well he told me about going into the Gucci store on Rodeo Drive and having a snooty sales clerk look down her nose at him as he was checking out the leather belts, so he hit back with: "Listen: don't dare treat me like that. *You* probably got the bus to work!"'

Then out of the blue I remembered something else and I turned to Cindy.

'By the way, I had letter from Dan just before I left London. He said to be sure and pass on his regards. He also asked me tell you that he still takes girls to LA for the weekend, but now he marries them first.'

You'll just have to take my word for it, I truly hadn't seen anything hidden deep in this message at the time of reading

Dan's letter—not until I saw the look on Cindy's face. In that instant I realised she must have once secretly gone to LA for the weekend with *my* boyfriend, when I was still in love and lust with him.

She raced off to the rest room and I followed her. Between sobs she yelled: 'Thanks for ruining my marriage.' Turns out that, despite her past denials, Mike had always had a suspicion about her having an affair with Dan, and now I'd inadvertently confirmed it.

I was upset I'd created havoc in leafy Connecticut, but more than that, I was overwhelmed at discovering Dan and Cindy had cheated on me. While I was regularly confiding in her about me and Dan, she'd snuck off with him for a dirty weekend. I had been betrayed big time.

That evening was pretty frosty all round, but in the morning Cindy and I both happened to get up early and we made our peace in the kitchen, with her swearing they hadn't had sex during the now-infamous weekend away. Yeah, right.

> *I suddenly had a vision of me as a shrivelled-up old prune by forty if I didn't develop the knack of bouncing back from disappointments and doublecrosses.*

In the immediate aftermath of finding out about their fling, I thought I was making a pretty good fist of forgiving. But down the track I realised I was still wounded and furious. Being deceived is the thing I like least in life. It took a few years before I let go of wanting to punish Cindy and Dan. Sadly they were wasted years in one sense; I'll never get them back.

3

PAYBACK, OR LET IT GO

I guess I'm a very slow learner when it comes to the big stuff. Thankfully I'm no longer an advocate for holding grudges. My new mantra is: Happiness is the best revenge. It beats the hell out of payback.

Okay, so forgiveness can help set us free. But we're all flawed. We won't always succeed right off the bat—either because our hearts aren't yet in the right place or because the person we want to forgive tells us to hit the road.

There are times when you'll fail at forgiving, but there's something to be said for doing your best.

A few years back I was doing a personal development course. During one session we were encouraged to think of someone who had wronged us, then to go home and ring them, announcing that all was forgiven. One young woman on the course selected her ex-husband, expecting a warm response. The ex had always ridiculed her interest in things such as reincarnation, likening her derisively to new-age screen icon Shirley MacLaine, who I and my friends all love to hate as Julia Roberts's cranky neighbour in *Steel Magnolias* when that classic movie comes up on cable TV. So she gets on the phone and goes, 'Hi, it's Melanie. I'm doing this personal development course and we've been told to think of someone we need to forgive and then make contact. I just want to say that I forgive you for all the terrible things you did to me when we were together.' Her ex burst out laughing and simply said: 'See you in the next lifetime, Shirley,' then slammed down the phone. Gee, you don't think he might have resented the fact that she was putting the emphasis on *his* shortcomings?

I can't recall who I chose, but I have a dim memory of being almost as unsuccessful. But you know what? I now figure that life's too short to beat up on yourself if the other party says 'get lost' when you attempt to clear the decks—or if you realise with a sinking heart that you still have work to do before you can let go of past hurts. But why not at least *try* forgiveness to clean the slate? There's nothing to lose.

As a young journalist, I timidly asked famous feminist, Germaine Greer, if she ever reacts to situations because of her early conditioning, rather than to what she now knows about women's rightful place in the world. She replied: 'Oh, I do that all the time—but half the joy is in the struggle.' I mention this because Germaine's approach could well be useful. There are times when you'll fail at forgiving, but there's something to be said for doing your best—and that your best is quite simply good enough.

4

SOMETIMES FORGIVENESS FINDS *YOU*

I know what you're thinking. Someone with my history of sticking the knife in and turning it has no place writing a book about forgiveness. But better me than someone who's never been tempted to do anything but turn the other cheek. At least I'm well placed to compare the angst of hating with the relief of letting it go. Here's how this project came about.

Not so long ago, I met up with a friend for a casual breakfast. I think of her as my guardian angel. Well, that's what she is—an incredibly spiritual and evolved human being, always with a comforting word and wise advice when the chips are down (which is not infrequent in my case). Even though there are great gaps of time when we mightn't see each other, I know she always sends me positive thoughts for my higher good.

When we meet, I suddenly start raving on about the importance of forgiveness. She works in publishing, and next I'm telling her she should commission someone to write a book on this subject because it could transform lives. She likes my suggestion; then when I get home something shifts in me. Along with becoming more enthusiastic about the idea by the minute, I feel increasingly territorial. *I* want to write it. I *need* to be the one to write it and, furthermore, drama diva that I am, I suspect I might just die of sadness if she gives the job to someone else. That's how much I long to do this. So I email her to that effect.

She soon reports back with interest from her company, then the whole thing goes on hold while she attends an international book fair. While she is gone I have an encounter that absolutely convinces me I am the one to write this book. It happens, of all things, at a medical appointment.

I needed to see a skin specialist. I remember Dr Adrianna Scheibner, who I hadn't seen in years, not since I interviewed her when she was riding high with her laser dermatology practice in Beverly Hills, California. At the time she had a wide range of patients, from Hollywood A-listers to kids who wanted to leave the gang lifestyle and their tattoos behind them.

Born in Czechoslovakia and raised in Australia, Adrianna earned a high profile for ground-breaking techniques to rejuvenate skin, as well as doing magical work correcting birthmarks, scars and stretchmarks, and erasing tattoos. She was a leader in her field and was invited to the US to teach her techniques there. Dr Arnold Klein, the highly-esteemed dermatologist in Hollywood, asked Adrianna to set up her practice near his office in Beverly Hills. He then introduced her to plastic and reconstructive surgeons and specialist physicians. Soon there were days when Dr Klein alone would refer as many as ten new patients to her. Adrianna's practice grew beyond her wildest imagination.

In this super-specialised field, she reached the pinnacle of success. As one newspaper article described her: 'Laser guru to the stars and a saviour to children and teenagers with disfiguring birthmarks or gang tattoos.' She was ecstatic, and completely engrossed in this artistic science. Then several years later the unthinkable happened.

This young, beautiful, talented, wildly successful doctor suffered a spectacular fall from grace and it was as though she vanished into thin air . . . until a winter's day when I needed to see a skin doctor.

Someone told me she was in practice again after a forced period in the wilderness. It took a lot of persistence to find out where her new premises were but then, finally, I secured an appointment. She walked into the waiting room and looked at me in utter surprise.

'Do you remember me?' I asked. She beamed: 'Finally!!! It took the universe some time to bring you to me! I have been looking for you for over a year. When I couldn't find you, I literally prayed for the universe to please bring you back into my life. I am not quite sure why I had this incredible urge, but we'll soon find out. I assure you, it's no coincidence you came here today.'

5

WHEN YOU LOSE EVERYTHING

Adrianna was cheated out of her money, reputation, and ability to earn a living by the finance professionals who were supposed to be looking after her interests. They embezzled her funds. She lost everything, and was reduced to living in a small car.

The enormity of the betrayal was spectacular—their grand finale being to arrange to have the media spotlight focused on Adrianna for all the wrong reasons. In a city where only winners have any currency, Adrianna was now seen as the loser of all losers. I had been greatly saddened at the time to read of her crash from a great height.

As we talked, I got on to my pet subject of forgiveness and the proposed book. Adrianna's face lit up:

But that's *my* story! It's all about forgiveness. The rewards of true and complete forgiveness are so enormous and so spectacular that if I'd known this, I'd have done it much sooner. And what's more, if everyone understood what they'd get if they truly forgave whoever has wronged them, they'd do it immediately, no matter how great the wrong. The result of even ten percent of the population truly forgiving would be nothing short of a complete transformation of the entire world as we know it! Can you imagine a world in which people are genuinely happy and living to their full potential? I can, and it can happen in our lifetime if someone explains how forgiveness works—and that someone is apparently you.

It was quite a moment, although one in which I seriously wondered whether I'd prove equal to this task, as envisaged so eloquently by Adrianna. I couldn't wait to share this development with my publisher on her return.

Contract signed, I decided to begin this adventure by interviewing Adrianna. I was attracted to the extremes of what had happened to her—being so spectacularly successful and then embezzled and shamed and losing so much—and how the act of forgiving her abusers had allowed her to rise from the ashes, better than ever. I set off by asking about those who harmed her and she was very frank, saying the truth is she harmed *herself.*

At the time I wasn't aware that it was the sum total of all the thoughts stored in my subconscious mind that attracted the people who manifested my greatest fears and aspirations. Nobody did anything to me I didn't permit them to do.

We all bring a whole cauldron of thoughts and concepts with us, even as infants. What we do with this incredibly huge reservoir of accumulated thoughts and counter-thoughts determines what happens to us.

The concept I had to get over was being a victim of betrayal. I re-enacted this right through my life. I had this expectation at some deep level that people would betray me—so they did.

I just looked at her and said 'Wow!' I was shocked, not just because of what she had said but because the reality of it clicked for me too. That had also been my way of viewing the world.

If everyone understood what they'd get if they truly forgave whoever has wronged them, then they'd do it immediately, no matter how great the wrong.

I moved my chair closer to hers and asked Adrianna to continue.

It's as though our minds act as a movie camera inside our heads. We project this to the world out there. Those actors who can match the script of our own movie are then drawn to us. They walk into the frame, and manifest the very things we believe. Because we're not aware our own thoughts determine what happens to us, we think it's other people who are evil and harm us. The real enemy and the only enemy is within. No-one can do anything to us unless we give them permission. By giving this permission we give others power over our lives.

The first and crucial step was to accept responsibility for my part in the drama. Immediately I became aware of just how much power I'd given away to others, specifically the people I'd allowed to victimise me. The resulting empowerment gave me more energy and allowed me to sleep better. I'd wake up rested and not feel like I'd just lived the torment of a gladiator's nightmare. And I didn't tire, even with long hours.

It's easy to say 'I don't want to be a victim any more', but to change one's thinking so profoundly that not a single thought of something going wrong ever occurs is a different matter. How many women insist, 'Okay, I don't want this kind of abusive relationship; I'll never do it again.' Next thing they attract the exact same kind of person. As the Buddha said: 'The greatest miracle is to change a single thought.'

6

VICTIM NO MORE

Adrianna felt such an urgency about the need to review her thinking, that it was as though her life depended on it, which it did, literally.

> I wanted to change, more than a drowning person wants to gasp for the life-giving breath of air. To get rid of the entire reservoir of old thinking patterns seemed like an impossible task. I just wanted to push a button that erased everything in one go. This is where the 12-step program, a set of guiding prinicples for recovery from addiction and other behavioural problems, came to my rescue. And in my case it was easy to admit I'd made a mess of my life.

Added to this, she had an unshakable faith in the intelligence and benevolence of the universe, so she made a decision to trust in this invisible power, and wholeheartedly handed over her life, mess that it was.

This can't be faked. Fake it till you make it doesn't work as far as God is concerned. True surrender and forgiveness can't be faked.

I have no doubt that it was because of my willingness to surrender that, one by one, the thoughts that had created my problems floated into my awareness. First and foremost was my attitude towards money. I realised I'd thought of money as dirty. Money was an impostor that intruded on, and certainly marred, what I considered sacred. To help people was my entire aim in life. Without that, my life was not worth living.

At the age of four in her native Czechoslovakia, Adrianna developed a severe rash on her face that was so disfiguring people treated her like a leper. It lasted three horrible years, and the end result was that she acquired empathy for anyone with a physical deformity—especially for those with facial or skin problems, in particular children.

I made a decision early on I'd become a doctor who fixed skin problems and helped people change from being miserable to happy. Carolyn Myss, an American medical intuitive and mystic, calls it being 'a wounded healer'. And I didn't think of being rewarded. I actually developed an aversion to anything to do with finance, as I considered it a privilege to be in a position to help.

And because I had this enormous aversion to money, I left the financial side of my thriving practice in Beverly Hills to a financial adviser and his staff.

This 'financial advisor', who we'll call Paul (not his real name), had just been released from serving a three-year gaol sentence for defrauding banks to the order of millions of dollars. His explanation about what happened was so plausible, and he was so frank about wanting to change his life, that Adrianna believed him.

> *True surrender and forgiveness can't be faked.*

Adrianna is very clever, so it's difficult to understand that, despite her foreboding, this man got away with six years of embezzling her funds. It wasn't until she showed her financial documentation to another accountant that she was alerted to the problem.

It's now clear that he, his family and his select friends, plus my own accountant, were all in cahoots. We tend to look at those who do things like that to us as baddies, but I have now detached enough to accept responsibility for my own thinking which created that situation, and to look at why Paul did what he did.

He loved his wife so much he made a commitment to take care of her no matter what. He was even prepared to go to gaol again. So in a curious way it was the right motivation. Unfortunately it resulted in harming both me, and all the people I could have helped. At least that's how it all appeared prior to my final, complete act of forgiveness.

7

FROM RIDING HIGH IN LA ...
TO ROCK BOTTOM

When Adrianna first arrived in the United States, it soon became obvious that not everyone could afford laser treatments. Even when birthmarks were quite disfiguring, many health insurance companies considered these life-transforming treatments to be cosmetic and refused to cover the costs. Many people didn't have any insurance, and heaps of them were children tormented by the cruelty of others. Knowing what this felt like, Adrianna decided to offer free treatments through The Brave Hearts Foundation, which she founded.

After gang riots in LA, she became aware of another huge need throughout the US: gang-related tattoos in kids and adolescents. If youngsters wanted to leave the gang culture and lead a normal life, they couldn't do so until these gang insignia were removed. She was in the process of raising money to open tattoo-removal clinics in LA, Chicago and Harlem and, if it hadn't been for the embezzlement, she could have easily funded these.

The crescendo came when my then-accountant announced I had to file for bankruptcy. There is no way to adequately describe how I felt when I was told my life's endeavour had suddenly come to an end. Not only did I spend my entire childhood daydreaming about what I was going to do when I grew up, but I spent my high school years studying every moment to make sure I would get into medical school. I went to only one party in the six years of high school and spent my summer holidays doing homework one year ahead. I mention all this just to give you a picture of what it took for me to reach the pinnacle of success in the field of cosmetic laser specialty.

My life involved sitting all day long, looking through magnifying glasses, going minutely over skin. I absolutely love doing the treatments—it's like painting or drawing in extreme—but dealing with patients while they are going through the healing process, however, is quite a different matter. I had to cope with their anxiety, engendered by the healing process, because they always looked worse before they looked better. And imagine doing that to famous people, whose faces were unrecognisable for weeks. They saw their careers as ruined and, no matter how carefully I described the healing process, patients didn't understand it until they were in it themselves. They'd panic, and I lived with the constant threat of lawsuits. Some even threatened to go to the press with photos when they looked their worst. I had to muster all my courage and call on God to give me the strength to keep on going.

Paul and his faithful mob used the circumstances of my being so completely absorbed in the work and having to hand-hold patients while they healed to run completely free with my money. Plus, as I did the work for the results I got for patients—not for money—it made what they were doing even easier for them.

As it happened, Adriana's file for bankruptcy was rejected on a technicality; however, by that stage, her life as she knew it was over. And she decided to end her life. She even rationally worked out how she would do it, and then, two weeks before D-day, a patient came in who was obviously shocked by her appearance.

She said, 'You look dreadful; what's the matter with you? Take your son and go to our house in Jamaica. You need a break.' I smiled and thanked her, but didn't take up the kind offer. I had made up my mind and I was going through with the termination of the nightmare. However, she turned up again and this time took charge: 'That's it! I'm calling my assistant right now. You're going to Jamaica.' She made the arrangements with such authority that I felt God, through this beautiful lady, had put an abrupt end to my deadly plans. I took it as divine intervention.

I didn't utter a single sound as Adrianna laid out what came next. I was spellbound.

The arrangements were made so quickly I forgot all about the large bottle of pills I intended to take to end my life. They were still in my handbag. While I was in Jamaica with my son, Aaron, at the holiday mansion of one of Hollywood's top producers and his wife, I looked through their guestbook. It was filled with the names of Hollywood's who's who and my mind started reeling. Now that I had nothing to do but think about what a mess I'd made of my life—as Paul had so cunningly led me to believe—I stared at these famous names, thinking, how can I ever face these people again? How can I face my son and myself? How can I face anyone, ever? And least of all my parents!

My mind went into overdrive. The most horrible thoughts of utter desolation attacked me, causing excruciating physical pain, as my adrenaline release was no doubt sky high. The thoughts came fast—each more fear-laden than the last. It was a perfect storm right inside my own head, so rapid and so horrible that I reached for my bag in a stupor and took two of the tablets. Nothing happened, so I took another three, then another five, then ten, plus I had two large glasses of vodka with a bit of orange juice to make it slightly more palatable, as I never drink spirits. It tasted and smelt so horrible I had to hold my nose shut so I wouldn't throw up. I kept on taking five to ten tablets with every sip of the alcohol. Over the fifteen minutes it took me to do all this I began to feel calmer. It was a relief to have my mind slow down, even a little.

An hour later, around 11 p.m., I finally felt sleepy and went to bed. I woke two hours later and sat upright . . . suddenly aware I wasn't breathing. I looked at the bottle on the bedside table. It was empty . . . I'd taken eight or nine thousand milligrams of pethidine [known as Demerol in the US]. That's enough to kill a horse and an elephant together. The amount of vodka was also large enough to give me alcohol poisoning, or at least make me lose consciousness.

I was in this beautiful mansion in a remote part of the island and all the servants had gone home; the place was empty, except for my seventeen-year-old son, asleep in another room. We had no car and the telephone was out, due to a storm. Even if I'd been able to get to a hospital it was too late to pump my stomach. Right then and there I surrendered myself utterly into God's hands.

There was no breath and no need to breathe, and I understood what it means that 'man does not live by bread alone'. I found myself in the spiritual dimension in which the body doesn't even exist, let alone breathe. In that state, breath is not needed. Spirit alone is everything in a very literal sense.

God saved me and, from a medical point of view, it was a miracle. I sat in bed all night, in complete clarity and crystal-clear awareness, apologising: 'God I didn't mean to do it. *please* forgive me.' I now understood that the spirit is what sustains all living creatures and that the body is nothing more than a lifeless husk. Despite the gravity of the situation, I laughed out loud at having forgotten this fact. It's knowing this that sets us free and I had simply clouded it out of conscious-awareness.

It became clear to me that night that it's possible to be completely and wholeheartedly in the spiritual world, and yet function in the material. It all depends on where we believe our treasure is. This experience gave me a spiritual awakening.

> *I now understand that the spirit is what sustains all living creatures and that the body is nothing more than a lifeless husk.*

8

PICKING UP THE PIECES

Adrianna returned to LA, grateful to be alive, and determined to give notice to all the conspirators—although her financial adviser managed to convince her she couldn't cope without him.

I still believed what they'd been telling me for years—that it was all my fault. Now to my horror I saw just how much they'd allowed my finances to become such a mess: I was months behind in rent and tax payments.

They had to figure an exit plan, which had consisted of getting me to file for bankruptcy and drive me to commit suicide. It almost succeeded. Before the bankruptcy was suggested, they'd had another plan: trying to get me to take out a life insurance policy for US$3 million. Paul wanted me to make my will, naming him as the executor. It was so obvious, but still I didn't get it. I was so naive and such a perfect victim! What kept me going then was that I'd been spending many of my weekends in gaol taking off gang-related tattoos, as part of my work for The Brave Hearts Foundation. This gave these young people a second chance. More and more my life had become miserable and I was stressed to the limit, but it was nothing compared to the horrors I heard from these young people. Sometimes I felt ashamed for even thinking my life was a living hell. In comparison with theirs, I lived in paradise.

Adrianna told me that Paul had become addicted to Demerol, and had made short work of a supply that came into the surgery while she was away on a break—he'd self-administered eight of the ten bottles.

I freaked out. 'What are you trying to do to me? If the Medical Board finds out, they'll pull my licence.' These words of mine presented him with a golden opportunity. First he spread the rumour I was addicted—and then his family went to the Medical Board to try and finish me off by lodging a complaint. Meanwhile they were not paying my taxes, so the tax office closed my practice down. From there things became so bad that I'd challenge any Hollywood writer to think up something more melodramatic.

That Christmas was the bleakest I'd ever experienced. My dark brown hair turned white from the stress and I was screaming and yelling at God, 'All I've done is help people—so why are you allowing this to happen?' In the overwhelming state of desperation, I wasn't aware it had been my own thinking that had done the damage.

Adriana's emotional pain was so severe that she finally did what the rumour was accusing her of doing: she took Demerol, to calm her battered mind. Shortly, however, her mind was anything but calm.

> I couldn't think rationally and I just wanted everything to go away. It did when I took Demerol, but only for a few hours. I took so much that it no longer worked, and I started to lose consciousness. There were times, when half-conscious, I became aware of Paul injecting me with what should have been lethal doses.

Another miracle was to come Adrianna's way.

> God took me by the scruff of my neck and saved me: I was invited to give a talk in Japan. I also had a friend who wanted me to open a clinic in the Middle East. She said, 'If you ever speak to him [Paul] again, I'll never talk to you. You have to make a choice: it's either me or him.' The decision was so easy I wondered what on earth had kept me so loyal to him for so long? So that's how it ended. She took me away and, thank God, I had zero withdrawal symptoms when I went to Japan.

9

FORGIVENESS CAN'T BE FAKED

During the next few years of exile, Adrianna spent the time largely practicing continuous surrender, which she found much harder than it sounds. Imagine not making any decisions or taking any actions to sustain your life; instead, relying totally on divine providence to come through. She told me it was like being a feather on the palm of God's hand, and being prepared to be moved whichever way the wind blows. As a result of this new way of living she realised just how many immovable concepts she'd acquired since childhood, and how these contributed to all that 'happened' to her.

> *It came down to a clear choice: peace and forgiveness . . . or being right, and resentful.*

I'd come to trust in the much bigger picture. And since I didn't need the majority of the thoughts which previously occupied my mind, I became quiet and peaceful. This resulted automatically in profound bliss—a happiness completely independent of any external happenings. It surpassed all understanding, and out of its depth came automatic forgiveness—first and foremost of myself. I had to forgive myself for having been so foolish.

Next came asking for forgiveness of everyone I'd knowingly or unknowingly harmed. I was surprised at the length of this list. I'd lived my life trying to help others, yet I now realised this help wasn't always in the best interest of these people, no matter how good my intentions. For example, my trust and generosity permitted Paul and the others to become thieves. Knowing this made it much easier to forgive them.

For the second time, Adrianna stressed to me that true forgiveness can't be faked. And that the trick is to forget the wrong as though it never happened—permanently. In fact, to not even see anything as 'wrong'.

In my life everything had gone wrong and been turned upside down. It takes years to build a reputation and moments to destroy it. In my field, a damaged reputation isn't easily forgotten, and mine had been completely destroyed. The immensity of what I had to forgive seemed too big. To forgive was like saying my life didn't matter, that it was okay to have destroyed it. I went over this question again and again. One thing was sure if I wanted to be forgiven, *I* had to forgive in turn . . . but sticking to that was a problem.

I could say to myself 'I forgive them all', and a few moments later remember how nice it would be to have even a fraction of the money I'd earned. But that isn't forgiveness!

There were times when resentment took over for hours. During these times I understood why I'd taken medication to get out of these bad feelings, and that righteous resentment is the most powerful poison known to mankind. It was poison I was drinking because of what someone else had done in the past, and in a strange way it felt good. That past wasn't retrievable and it involved people who weren't concerned about me at all and who were probably at this moment enjoying their life, having forgotten all about me. There was a moment of clarity when I understood that part of my mind was addicted to the bad feelings that came with being a victim. What a revelation that was!

It came down to a clear choice: peace and forgiveness . . . or being right and resentful. I wish I could say it was easy and that I made it immediately—the battle between good and evil and just letting it all go occupied so much of my time and energy (it was a good thing I wasn't working just to earn a living). Day after day I spent time and energy on this and it was hard going. I realised just how powerful and overwhelming thoughts were. It resembled the never-ending fight between Neo and Mr Smith in *Matrix*. No sooner did one lot of thoughts subside than another hundred took their place.

In the end it took complete determination, vigilance and continuous appeal to God to please take it all away. I wanted peace of mind more than I wanted justice or revenge.

The outcome for Adrianna was that peace was won, and she let her embezzlers and their accomplices go scot-free. She says it wasn't until the forgiveness was complete that the peace returned—and with it came total contentment.

My theory is that genuine forgiveness, issued for its own sake, has a way of giving back unexpected collateral benefits. Well in Adrianna's case, the riches that came her way include a multitude of discoveries, which are major advances in the field of laser dermatology.

> The first was a way of treating [ageing skin], in which the laser light is able to result in on-the-spot rearrangement of collagen so that wrinkles disappear immediately, without the overlying skin being removed. Imagine instant and complete disappearance of wrinkles while the skin remains cool to the touch, and the healing period is reduced to less than two weeks. This alone is nothing short of miraculous.
>
> I attended a meeting of the American Academy of Dermatology at which Professor Rox Anderson, Head of the Wellman Laboratories, which are part of Harvard Medical School—there is no higher authority—always gives a talk on the future developments in the field of lasers. I had been doing for some years what Professor Anderson presented as a theoretical possibility. After his speech I showed him the results I'd been getting, which by the way also made it possible to treat scars immediately after surgery. 'Is this what you mean, Rox?' I asked him. He just smiled: 'It's great to see you back in the saddle. I guess now you want me to explain how what you are doing works.' 'Absolutely. I can't explain it, I can just do it.'

How many scientists are looking for an effective and fast way of growing hair, treating scars, stretchmarks, reducing pore size and in general keeping skin eternally youthful and perfect in appearance? Creativity is the outcome of a mind free from old concepts.

Today I understand I had the greatest of fortunes to find myself in the greatest of misfortunes. The result was that after trying everything I was capable of, my mind came to a full stop, like hitting a brick wall. I found myself utterly alone, homeless, my reputation destroyed, my livelihood destroyed and my beautiful dream shot to pieces. The way out came with surrender. It felt like walking off the edge of the Grand Canyon with nothing to hold me up. The nightmare had all taken place in my own mind.

It was like an actor awakening from a part which they'd mistaken to be their own real life, into a state in which forgiveness had no meaning because there's no-one to forgive.

During our talk I told Adrianna I believed forgiveness is a good thing, as long as it doesn't mean you have to condone what they did, or agree to have dinner with that person ever again.

'No, you're wrong! True forgiveness sets you free to the point where you *want* to have dinner with them, and are at peace with what was done. And actually that's exactly what I did as soon as the forgiveness was complete. I knocked on the door of Paul, my one-time nemesis, and invited myself in for a cup of tea. I can't even describe the feeling of freedom which came as a result of the victory over my own mind.'

Adrianna's face now literally shines with the joy that comes from bearing no grudges and loving everyone . . . herself included. Forgetting the past is a small price to pay for all these treasures.

I would say her advice to others on this path can best be summed up this way:

- Begin by digging deep to figure out what it is you're not seeing that is causing dysfunctional behaviour.
- Be authentic in terms of forgiving yourself and others.
- Surrender to the process and it will take on a life of its own.
- And, if humanly possible, take out some quiet time to listen with your heart and just go with the flow.

Then watch what happens!

10

IS REVENGE THE ULTIMATE ORGASM?

Adrianna's heroic journey makes letting go of the blame game sound like a no-brainer, but so many of us are still back at Forgiveness 101. Much as we might ache for a happy, calm life, it's often two steps forward and one step back for new players. I'm not going to lie to you. The truth is, plotting revenge in the immediate aftermath of being wronged is downright orgasmic. The problem is, we can become hooked on that emotional response and 'reward', and therein lies the seductive road to hell.

I know of two young women who had been at school together and later married best buddies. By chance they found out at pretty much the same time that their husbands were playing around. They linked arms and went to a bar where they drank way too many cocktails and dreamt up a plan to join forces to punish, in spades, their naughty husbands. Humiliate and trick the bastards, then life will be good again, was their scheme—and it worked, up to a point. Unfortunately, when all was said and done, the only people who came out ahead were the lawyers.

Confucius hit the nail on the head with this chilling warning: 'If you're planning revenge, first dig two graves.' It says it all, does it not? One grave for the person we want to get back at, the another for us.

Punishing the other party is definitely one way to react when someone else has done the wrong thing. But is it the *best* way? Deep, deep down we know that it is not, because that's all about a quick hit of vindictiveness, which will inevitably be followed by further damage—not for them, but for us. Soon the other party will rise above the annoyance of you or I who, in a fit of rage, let their tyres down or vexatiously put their name on a herpes website . . . and *we'll* remain stuck in that withered place of being a sleazy dude. Even if no-one ever finds out for sure that it was us who did these mean-spirited things, the fact is that *we* know, and that's what really matters. Robert Louis Stephenson wrote that 'ultimately we all sit down to a banquet of consequences', and who wants a bitter feast?

> *Plotting revenge in the immediate aftermath of being wronged is downright orgasmic.*

My God, between Robert Louis Stephenson and Confusius we've got all the proof we need . . . yet to forgive is soooo hard. I must come clean, I really hated letting go of the 'Get even, and *then* forgive' philosophy—even though I knew the time had come. It made so much sense for a while there, because it was like having a bet each way. Surely I'd still get into heaven by the skin of my teeth—but I got to be a vengeful bitch first, which was divine. Yes, it *was* fleetingly divine, but it can easily become a case of enjoy now, pay later.

Once I finally cotton on to one of life's major truths I figure there's no turning back; and in the case of forgiveness, I can now no longer go back and pretend that it's okay for a woman to cut up her ex's favourite suit into small pieces as retaliation for him playing around. It's dumb and childish, and real grown-ups just shouldn't do stuff like that.

Old habits die hard though, and occasionally an evil payback thought will rear its ugly head. Here's what I do when this happens: I force myself to imagine I'm standing on the other side of the room, watching my antics, and I say, with as much contempt as I can muster: 'Oh look, the stupid idiot's doing it again.'

It works every time, breaking the mood.

Part two
MIRACLES HAPPEN

11

MIRACLES HAPPEN!

A giant turning point for me came not long ago, when I reconnected with my child's father after an acrimonious absence of years. Our last meeting had ended on a sour note. In the intervening years I found it impossible to let go of my regret. I continued to take a dim view of things he had said and done, whilst devoting even more energy to castigating myself for that final encounter—replaying it over and over and thinking of a thousand 'if onlys'.

I should add that this did not overtly get in the way of the rest of my life, but there always remained an underlying sadness and a craving on my part for an acceptance between us that bubbled away beneath the surface of everything else I did and thought.

A chance came along, offering an opportunity to find him again, and I decided to run with it. From there it took a couple of weeks of hard work to track down his phone number, in what turned out to be a remote location. I had to keep reminding myself to breathe as I contemplated how our conversation would go, given so much was riding on it. All I knew for sure was that this opportunity had arrived at a time when at last I was close to letting both of us off the hook. I guess fate was being kind in a way by delaying our shot at a reunion.

I wish to protect my son's privacy, and that of his father, as regards to what exactly happened when the three of us did eventually meet up, but I will tell you that, by going into this with an open heart, I found it was a great deal easier than it would otherwise have been. And much more enjoyable.

The star of it all was young Charlie, who blew us, his parents, away by being incredibly gracious. There was a complete absence of malice and ill-will on his part. And by observing him in that moment, I finally understood the final piece of the jigsaw: that there was nothing to forgive.

I had been given quite a gift. A light had finally been switched on in my brain, bringing with it the knowledge that I needed to release everyone I'd ever held a grudge against. I learnt that from my amazing son, on what was one of the best nights of my life.

> *This opportunity had arrived at a time when at last I was close to letting both of us off the hook.*

12

FORGIVING DOESN'T HAVE TO MEAN YOU'LL BE BEST BUDDIES

I've done enough self-sabotaging over the years to be a world expert on what this can do to a person, and it sure comes a poor second to the contentment that results from throwing away one's voodoo dolls—literally or figuratively. Having said that, it will most likely take a couple of reincarnations before I'm as evolved as Adrianna, to the point where I can eventually condone the offences of everybody I forgive, but it's an interesting idea.

Interesting, but is it a necessary add on to the process of releasing yourself from the torture of wanting revenge, along with the debilitating effects of actively despising? Maybe the truth lies somewhere in between.

Surely there's nothing wrong with continuing to dislike someone, even though you've forgiven them. If you genuinely don't like him or her, why on earth would you want to have dinner with them? Will being that magnanimous bring us closer to heaven? Adrianna insists it's a higher level of forgiveness, and she's probably right, but I figure it will be my next lifetime before I get my head around that one.

I know I shouldn't be treating this important topic like a plate of pastries and only taking those I like, but you can only do what you can do, and no amount of good intentions will make you a saint if your heart isn't in it. You first have to have the will.

And there's no law that says you have to *verbalise* forgiveness. You'll recall my acquaintance who contacted her ex-husband to tell him she was no longer angry about all the rotten things he'd done to her during their marriage, with no mention of her own shortcomings. He was not impressed. In fact he thought she was a complete fruit cake. So time over, she might do better to offer up *silent* forgiveness rather than picking up the phone.

Being seriously neurotic, and fearing that I'm easily forgettable, I have this recurring nightmare in which I ring some generic guy and launch into a speech about how I'm finally at a place where I can wipe the slate clean with regard to his long-ago misdemeanours, and he says to me, 'Do I know you?' Don't laugh; it could happen—and then I'd have something new to hold a grudge about.

> There's no law to say you have to verbalise forgiveness.

It would be much safer in some cases to dispatch your messages of forgiveness in a non-verbal manner, either by attempting to communicate on a spiritual level or by seeking the person out and just being in their space in a loving, nonjudgmental way. Keep in mind a warm hug can say so much—especially if you linger over it. They won't fail to pick up on what you're telling them, and they will smile. Probably.

13

WE ALL HAVE UNFINISHED BUSINESS

Increasingly, I like to make use of the quiet moments before sleep to have imaginary conversations with people with whom I have unfinished business. It sounds weird, but it can be sooooo healing. There's often great intensity in these one-sided chats, or in letters you write with emotion and which you have no intention of posting. I sometimes find that breakthroughs come about in the silence, making it unnecessary to engineer a face-to-face confrontation.

I just want to say one other thing here about the benefits that can flow from letting go of resentment—so long as it's done willingly and with good grace. I fully understand that it should be carried out, first and foremost, because it's the right thing to do—but in my fledgling career as a forgiver, I'm increasingly finding that there are collateral rewards. Here's an example from my own life.

During the tantalising weeks when I was trying to track down the phone number for my son's father, I was at a wake after a funeral. A close friend of mine made an inappropriate comment about me in front of people we both hold in high esteem. I was upset, storming out of the wake. She emailed me the next day, begging for forgiveness and explaining that she hadn't been herself, given she was in the grip of grief (plus she'd had quite a few champagnes).

> *I sometimes find that breakthroughs come about in silence.*

I thought about the incident in quite a calm way and saw clearly I had a choice. I could tell her to fuck off and that I didn't want anything more to do with her, or I could focus on the years of her kindness and loyalty, mindful that I'm blessed to have her as my pal. So . . . I emailed back and told her, 'Yes, you hurt me, but let's put it behind us.'

Now I realise it's a pretty unremarkable story, but I tell it because of what came next. I hit an unexpected roadblock in my search for that elusive phone number—and she was the only person I could think of who's an irresistible sweet-talker, and tenacious enough, to ring the roadblock and help progress the search. She's such a beautiful person she gladly agreed to carry out this delicate task. I'm convinced that, without her intervention, I would never have been successful. I'll always remember, too, that had I refused to overlook her rudeness the day before, I wouldn't have been able to ask for help.

I now feel closer to her than ever. Friends for life.

14

BEING STUCK IN NON-FORGIVENESS

It has become abundantly clear to me that it's only the elite few, the straight-A forgivers, who manage to find it in their hearts to let go of bitterness *and* progress to happily sharing a meal with those who caused their suffering.

At the other end of the spectrum are those who are firmly stuck in non-forgiveness and wouldn't dream of inviting the offender over for a barbecue as a way to bury the hatchet. So where does that leave this second group? Is there any hope of attaining enlightenment?

I just hope God realises that it's not always a breeze letting bygones be bygones . . . because old habits die hard. Take romance. Sometimes rejection and betrayal hurt so much that for a while it may seem the only way to ease the pain is to destroy the person who did the cheating, along with wrecking the good name of their latest lover, your replacement—especially if your seat is still warm. Problem is, once you've tasted blood it can be hard to stop, to know where to draw the line.

One tale which has always fascinated me surrounds Nobel Prize-winning playwright, Harold Pinter, who left home for a gorgeous blonde biographer, Antonia Fraser. Pinter's abandoned wife, actress Vivien Merchant, was quoted in a London newspaper, making fun of Fraser's very large feet, pointing out that she would be able to wear Pinter's shoes. It was a petty comment and hardly award-winning vindictiveness, but it's not hard to imagine her public humiliation. It's only human, and it probably felt this was the only chance she had to claw back some of her power.

Once you've tasted blood, it can be hard to stop, to know where to draw the line.

As a young journalist I attended a media conference to promote a movie in which Merchant co-starred. She was an incredibly interesting actress and it was a thrill to be in her presence. Little did any of us know that she was unravelling. By later accounts (including her own), she was unable to come to terms with having been tossed over for the glamorous Antonia Fraser. This sad story ends with Merchant's alcoholic death at fifty-three.

This tragedy is the classic example of the one who was dumped becoming all bitter and twisted, and losing any chance at joy. Her husband, who did the disappearing act, apparently did not look back, enjoying a wonderful second marriage.

It's way too late for Vivien Merchant, but the message comes through loud and clear to anyone who finds themselves in that leaky boat: get a life!

15

WHEN WORK IS HELL

The same goes when things unravel on the work front. As an exceptionally clever person once pointed out (and the rest of us have been repeating it ever since), no-one on their death bed is going to wish they'd spent more time at the office. After all, it's just a place you go between nine and five. It doesn't define who you are. It's only a job. And the *really* important time to keep this in mind is when you're being treated indifferently by the boss or by a co-worker.

Being passed over for a promotion that promises the corner office, plus more money, makes it quite tempting to despise both the boss and the employee who beat you to that cushy higher rung on the corporate ladder. But sometimes you're genuinely not the best candidate—or just maybe you didn't make your ambitions clear enough.

I once met an executive at a charitable organisation, and she knew I was acquainted with a board member there. She took the opportunity to complain about not being elevated to a recent vacancy on the board. She bitched on and on, telling me she'd been the obvious choice.

I later recounted this conversation to the board member I knew, who demonstrated no sympathy for the loser.

'Did she put her hand up to be the replacement?'

'Well no', I said. 'Apparently she just presumed they'd pick her.'

'Oh really? Well it doesn't work like that. You have to be pro-active in life and put your hand up.'

Good point.

I'll tell you something else I've discovered—life being the cosmic joke it is—if you work with someone who seems determined to make things miserable for you and is causing trouble for you with the boss, there's no point switching jobs. You'll only end up having your very own *Groundhog* moment, because that person in another form will be waiting for you at the new place. Better to rise above the irritation. Be nice to them, act as if there's nothing to forgive. Trust me, there'll soon be a change to your advantage. Either that person will be transferred to the Lapland branch, or else the troublemakers may warm towards you.

At a paper I once wrote for there were two women who were determined to wear me down by being truly horrible. I imagine their intention was to force me into leaving. I'll die wondering why they hated me, but they did, and I fought back with relentless courtesy, as though I didn't notice their spitefulness. I just kept smiling, and it threw them off guard, which gave me the mental edge to hang in there. Then out of the blue I was transferred to another section of the paper. No, not the Lapland bureau, but to a department on another floor, and that was far enough away.

It was during that pretty crappy time I figured out something else. The reality that not everyone is going to like you is actually not a drama. It's not a situation that urgently needs to be turned around. If someone hates you, well, that's just the way it is, and it's stupid to respond to hate with more hate and a yen for revenge.

> *If you work with someone who seems determined to make things miserable for you and is causing trouble for you with the boss, there's no point switching jobs.*

It all seems so petty in hindsight doesn't it? Something to laugh about. So why not speed up the process and laugh while it's going on? Although if there's criminal behaviour at play, such as sexual harassment, then that's another matter entirely, and you shouldn't have to take that on the chin. No-one should.

Stay with me, though, because I have another theory about missing out on promotions. I've seen mates of mine in tears because plum jobs they wanted went to colleagues who had been prepared to sleep with the boss or, at the very least, flirt outrageously and wear low-cut blouses to the office. You know what? Things belong to the people who want them most. And if playing the seductress in the office is not a game you're willing to stoop to, then as far as I'm concerned, you won after all.

As I cast my mind back over my career so far, I reluctantly accept that I have always had a problem forgiving colleagues who got pay rises or opportunities, over and above what came my way. The reason I've been reluctant to accept this deep flaw is that I'm so ashamed. It's human nature at its most pathetic.

I swear to God I'm not trying to talk my way out of this, but I reckon what's going on here is that I grew up believing there's not enough love, money and praise to go round. It's a common neurosis and I think that's why I've always been so envious of others who get lucky at work and romance. Or maybe I've just been a jealous bitch.

A week ago I read about a survey which revealed that, for most people, our sense of happiness is not so much hitched to how much *we* earn but rather on what others of similar age and education are earning. A sense of deprivation sets in if the comparison doesn't favour us. It's the 'better than/worse than' game. '*Her* boyfriend is nicer looking than mine/*His* car is newer than mine/*Her* Christmas bonus is bigger than mine.'

Whether it's on the employment scene or in matters of the heart, our best shot at happiness comes from finally looking at our own lives and saying, 'this will do'. And at the same time silently sending good wishes to those whose own stars are on the ascendant.

16

HAPPINESS IS THE BEST REVENGE

If revenge is called for, then happiness is the ideal way to do it. Though it's dangerous to rush headlong into a new relationship just to try and prove a point, which is a trick played out in Hollywood all the time. Hey, I wonder if celebs who have notched up three, four and five divorces amass a combined seething towards the various spouses who walked out on them? That would be more time-efficient than loathing all the ex-partners individually, year after year, I guess.

It doesn't do any of us credit that we treat the misfortunes of the rich and famous as entertainment. This has become one of our main spectator sports. It's weird. We think we know what's in the hearts of stars we've never met, based merely on magazine beat-ups about ugly relationship break-downs, quoting nameless 'insiders' and 'sources'. But how could we?

I've not even been in the same room as the women I'm about to spotlight in this and the next chapter, let alone discussed with them their most private thoughts, so I'm not privy to anything the rest of community doesn't know (or thinks it knows). But when it comes to the topic of scorned women evening the score, they are worthy of mention . . .

If revenge is called for, then happiness is the ideal way to do it.

First up is former supermodel Christie Brinkley, who made headlines when she elected to have an open court as she fought her unfaithful husband, Peter Cook, for custody of their two young children and the division of property. She won—but at what price?

For a start, the youngsters will find out about the seedy details of Cook's ex-curricular activities as revealed in court and will one day understand the impact of their mother choosing to have an open hearing into these highly private matters. Unsavoury details of Cook's sex life came to light during proceedings—within hours the whole world knew of his affair, and of his love of porn—which may have been just what Brinkley had planned.

Cook's attorney said to Brinkley in court, 'You wanted this trial so you could publicly flog your husband', when he noted that she had supported keeping the trial public.

Also memorable is something a court-appointed psychiatrist, Dr Stephen Herman, said. When questioned by the children's attorney, Dr Herman declared Brinkley needs therapy as 'an outlet for her anger and feeling of betrayal' by her unfaithful husband.

In the end she got the real estate and the kids, and her ex was humiliated into the bargain. Big win all round for Christie

Brinkley. But you can't help wondering what the karmic kickback is likely to be for any of us who place revenge above all else.

The guy who wrote, 'God said, "Take what you want, and then pay for it",' was right.

17

END OF THE AFFAIR

Pretty much at the same time, golfing legend Greg Norman married tennis great, Chris Evert. In the process of the news about the Norman/Evert affair getting out, Laura Norman lost her husband of thirty years *and* her friend, Chris Evert. A double whammy of the worst kind, played out in the press, which compounded the humiliation for Mrs Norman, who shortly after the divorce rebranded herself as Laura Andrassy. She may or may not be finding enormous comfort in the US$107 million settlement she received after slugging it out in a blaze of publicity with her ex.

It's a stack of money in anyone's language, and she might have been well-advised to immediately make a beeline for a new beginning . . . maybe even a new love interest, but no. The former Mrs Norman reportedly then went for a share of the money the lovebirds were paid for the exclusive shots of their mega-nuptials in the Caribbean. It seems Laura's was not going to go quietly into the sunset, or quickly.

This is easy for me to say, as I'm not the one who was jilted here. But if only a couple of her gal pals had taken her out for a martini or three and pointed out that she's well-rid of a man who would cheat on her with one of their friends. Furthermore, would you want back a man who showed he's not overly endowed with class and sensitivity by straightaway marrying the other woman in an extravagant wedding, and securing a magazine deal to cover the event? Second weddings held indecently close to a hurtful divorce should be small and discreet. It's as simple as that, and Laura Norman-Andrassy's anger is understandable. Not helpful, but understandable.

> She might have been well-advised to immediately make a beeline for a new beginning.

On the other side of the Atlantic, Sir Paul McCartney did battle in court with his short-time wife, Heather Mills, who was trying to shake him down for close to US$150 million, by telling horror stories to the judge about how the former Beatle had allegedly treated her. The upshot was that she was awarded 'only' US$52 million. As she was about to leave the court room, she threw a glass of water over Sir Paul's lawyer, so it's probably fair to conclude that Mills isn't taking the verdict on the chin.

Memo to Heather: it isn't a good idea to badmouth an icon as adored as Paul McCartney—it is bound to backfire.

We can't read their minds, but it doesn't sound as though Christie, Laura and Heather will let go of their rage any time soon.

18

HAPPY ENDINGS AGAINST THE ODDS

Back on planet Earth, the financial stakes aren't usually in the millions when love goes bad, but emotions runs just as high. And sometimes the urge for retribution knows no limits. But would *you* go as far as Lynette Quessy, the vengeful wife who tried to harm her cheating husband by sprinkling crushed glass on his lunches?

As it came out in court (yes, she got caught), the wife had used a meat tenderiser to grind up glass from a fluorescent light bulb, keeping the particles in a plastic container in the pantry, ready for use. She blended the glass with the butter she spread on his sandwiches, and managed to do this five times before the jig was up and she was arrested.

Interestingly, her husband's affair after twenty years of marriage had been discovered three years earlier. They remained living together, in separate rooms, for the sake of their children. It was only when a property dispute between them was in full swing that her husband, Tim Nash, chipped his tooth on a chicken sandwich she had made.

Sometimes the urge for retribution knows no limit.

A week later, he noticed what looked like rock salt on his biscuits. He realised it was glass, and the same thing happened next day. Being a smart guy, he stopped eating the food she prepared and began keeping it in a freezer in his garage for later analysis.

The court heard Mr Nash called police only after he found a note in his wife's handwriting, inquiring what would happen to the transfer of their joint property should one of them die. Glass sandwiches, property transfer . . . it didn't look good.

Thankfully, her husband had escaped serious injury but what do you think happened here? Nope, you're wrong. It's had a happy ending.

Quessy pleaded guilty just before going to trial on one count of administering a poison and four counts of attempting to administer a poison. In sentencing, the judge said, 'You admitted that you wanted to hurt your husband . . . and that revenge was a thought in your mind . . . It could have resulted in internal laceration and bleeding', but then concluded Quessy was unlikely to reoffend and was previously of exemplary character.

The judge made reference to Mr Nash having lifted an apprehended violence order against his wife a while back, which had allowed her to return home after he'd testified earlier he no longer feared her.

Quessy got off with a nine-month suspended sentence and, after leaving court, returned immediately to the family home. She and her husband were reunited!

It appears both had done some serious forgiving.

19

SECRET ROMANCE IN A WARDROBE

Here's the thing . . . with revenge—if one gives in to that temptation—the secret is to know when to give it away and go back to being a rational human being. Which brings me to Ivana Trump, who delivered the punchline in the movie *First Wives Club*: 'Remember girls: don't get mad . . . get everything.'

What I like about Ivana Trump is that she presents in real life as a woman who was cheated on big-time and was initially disempowered. Yet, while she remained hostile for a little while, she was savvy enough with come up with another act for her life story. And it's one that seems to have brought her fulfilment. I'd certainly like to think so, because I figure she's one cool lady, and a winner to boot.

We all have to do things in our own time, and if this process takes a while, well it takes a while. It's how we finish that matters. For instance, I'm impressed by the leap of faith Jenny Ryan took in finally forgiving what many parents would consider the unforgivable.

Jenny's teenage daughter, Natasha, had run away from home, and for five years hid in the bungalow of her boyfriend, Scott Black, disappearing into a wardrobe when visitors came around.

The secret is to know when to give it away and go back to being a rational human being.

The Ryan family believed Natasha was dead, but how can you grieve properly when there's no body to bury? Then the story took a bizarre twist (as if it wasn't bizarre enough already) when someone randomly admitted to murdering Natasha. It was during the murder trial that police told the judge that thanks to a tip-off they had found Natasha alive and well.

Scott Black went to gaol for a year for perjury. Natasha, by now eighteen, returned to live with her mother, Jenny, who was both relieved and angry. If she was your daughter, you wouldn't know whether to hug or slap her, would you?

Somehow the young lovers' relationship survived, and six years after she emerged from hiding, they married in a romantic ceremony. On their big day, attended by both Natasha's parents, Mrs Ryan was quoted as saying that while she'll never forget the betrayal of her daughter allowing her to believe she was dead, she has forgiven her.

Part three

IT'S OFFICIAL . . .

20

IT'S OFFICIAL: FORGIVENESS IS GOOD FOR YOU

The research community has gone up in my estimation as I learn about academics investigating the significance of real forgiveness in keeping your body, mind and spirit in good working order. What else could be more important for the white coat brigade to explore? They're proving in controlled environments a link between health and the ability to forgive. Surely that's just as exciting as a major breakthrough in something of a purely physiological nature.

This kind of research has been a speciality of Kathleen Row, Chair of the Psychology Department at East Carolina University, for a decade now, and her findings have aired in a PBS documentary titled, *The Power of Forgiveness*. (It went on to win Best Film award at the Sun Valley Film Festival, and it's a buzz to think Row's significant work has been honoured in this way.) Row's results, in black and white, show a clear difference in the blood pressure and heart rate recovery levels of those who can forgive more easily, compared to those who can't. And there's a double whammy, as Row has shown forgiveness can yield positive benefits not only for the forgiver, but for the forgiven too.

Row gets participants to answer written questions about forgiveness. Then, in a private consultation, the participant, hooked up to heart rate and blood pressure monitors, is asked to think about a time he or she had been wronged.

'One finding is that people with a more forgiving personality will struggle to tell a story about a time when someone hurt them', she said. 'Other people will say, "Where do you want me to start?"' She noted the latter group's blood pressure and heart rates went up as they talk about being betrayed, while the vital signs of those who had forgiven the wrongdoing they were recalling showed a marked difference by returning more quickly to normal levels. And, interestingly, Row found older people are more likely to be forgiving, and that women are more likely to be forgiving in general than men.

Researchers, as well as everyday people, are finally wising up to something wonderful: there is a physiological and psychological purpose to forgiveness—good health and happiness.

> *Forgiveness can yield positive benefits not only for the forgiver, but for the forgiven too.*

I have also tracked down an account of studies being funded by an outfit called the Templeton Forgiveness Research Campaign. Their aim is to monitor and measure the physiological effects of forgiveness and its benefits. What I read was just as exhilarating as the findings of Kathleen Row. The bit that knocked my socks off was the account of the campaign's director, Everett Worthington, having his own capacity for forgiveness tested in an unimaginable manner.

He had literally just mailed off his manuscript outlining a step-by-step process for forgiveness, and then his own mother was murdered. You can bet *that* life challenge and how to deal with it wasn't included in his forgiveness manual! He admits that in the immediate aftermath of this brutal murder he noticed a baseball bat and said: 'I wish that whoever did this was here right now. I would beat his brains out.'

Somehow he found the inner-strength to practise what he preached. He managed to put the emphasis on what he considered the most important component of forgiveness—empathy. In his case, for the burglar who killed his mother. Worthington, as best as he could, went inside the mind of this killer, trying to understand how it might have happened.

'I can imagine what it must have been like for this kid to hear behind him a voice saying something like, "What are you doing here?"' he said. In doing so, he says he's been able to forgive his mother's murderer.

'I cannot imprison him by holding unforgiveness towards him.'

Meanwhile at Hope College in Michigan, researchers have been measuring heart rates, sweat rates and other responses of subjects asked to remember past slights.

'Their blood pressure increases, their heart rate increases, and their muscle tensions are also high', explained Professor Charlotte van Oyen Witvliet. This suggests their stress responses are greater during their unforgiving than forgiving conditions.

Scientists elsewhere have found that forgiveness has a lot to do with genetics. Research in chimpanzees shows it might even be crucial for survival of the species.

'In a cooperative system, it is possible that your biggest rival is someone who you will need tomorrow', said Frans De Waal of Emory University's Yerkes Primate Center. While the work at the Primate Center is intriguing, it's in another ballpark to the school of thought that promotes forgiveness for the peace of mind it's likely to deliver. One's about basic survival and the other is focused on the health and spiritual benefits.

Which matters more: survival or health benefits? I'll take both.

21

STARTING OVER

I assure you I'm not being judgmental about folks who hang on to their intense dislike for those they once loved because, in the end, when bad things happen, we all do what it takes to stop us from going crazy. But we don't always make wise choices under extremely emotional conditions, when we're in shock at having been played for a fool. We'd probably give everything we own just to be able to take back a cutting remark or a vicious action made in haste.

The big question is this: Is choosing not to forgive ever the right thing to do?

Over the past year I'd come to believe the answer is 'no' . . . until I heard about a remarkable individual, Ingrid Polson. Her estranged husband killed her two small children, her father, Peter Polson, then himself. Prior to wiping out Ingrid's entire family, her husband had, earlier in the day, tied up Ingrid and raped her. It was when she was at the hospital after this assault that he carried out the killings.

These are extreme circumstances in which I imagine even Mother Teresa would have found her faith sorely tested. And no doubt Ingrid's suffering has been intensified, given this man can never be brought to earthly justice.

> *We don't always make wise choices under extremely emotional conditions.*

When a radio broadcaster, Luke Bona, interviewed Ingrid Polson, I felt nothing short of privileged as I listened to her talk about her odyssey, and where it has taken her in emotional terms. I froze for a second when I heard Luke ask her whether it's possible to forgive and forget. Would she say 'Yes' or 'No'?

'I think it's possible to decide to move on in whichever way you choose to do that,' said Ingrid. 'Forgiveness is one of those topics I'm a little unsure about, because when things like this happen we are encouraged to forgive those who have trespassed against us, but sometimes what has happened is unforgiveable, and it's okay not to forgive—as long as you're not bitter and twisted. It's reasonable to say, "I can't forgive, but I'm continuing on".'

Wow! Ingrid is wise and brave, and, against the odds, she's a survivor. These days she seeks joy. Her words and actions show just how resilient the human spirit can be. In a world that hurls lavish praise on sports people and sitcom stars, there are those like Ingrid Polson who have done truly super-human things in the aftermath of great tragedy.

Ingrid will not forgive the man who raped her and murdered her family . . . but you know something, she found a path through the horror to a place that is right for her and, in the process of moving forward, she has wrestled back her power and discovered a new way to be happy. It's nothing short of inspiring.

22

WIRED FOR BLISS

I was watching Larry King one night on CNN when he devoted an entire program to how the mind works. All the guests were compelling contributors to the conversation, but Candace Pert PhD stood head and shoulders above the rest when she said: 'We are naturally hard-wired for bliss.'

I yelled at the TV set: 'Who is this woman???' I so wanted to believe Candace Pert because, if she's right, then this is practically the best news I'd ever heard, second only to finding out I was pregnant with my son.

I've read fifty million self-help books, participated in heaps of courses that promised to turn my life around, and endured two years of obscenely expensive psychotherapy but, through all of that, I somehow never got the memo about us being hard-wired for bliss. I've been under the misapprehension that life is no picnic, that's just the way it is, and I thought the best we can hope for after years of painful work is self-acceptance, with some individual moments of joy from time to time, if we're lucky.

Then along comes Candace Pert with her one-liner. This changed everything for me, especially as I've since found out that she has a scientific background—Johns Hopkins trained, no less. I really liked Candace Pert. Seeing her on Larry King, I came to the conclusion that she's the sort of person us girls would and could trust with our secrets. I'm convinced she wouldn't lie about something this important.

Now that I know we are definitely programmed to be joyful, it follows we'd be foolish to get in the way of what's rightfully ours. So refusing to forgive ourselves or others, and feeling wretched for years because someone else won't forgive *us*, well that's just plain stupid. I learnt from my new best friend, Candace Pert, that misery is not what the universe had in mind for any of us.

Brad, a twenty-five year old I know, went to Weight Watchers for a few months. I loved it when he'd tell me about the encouraging group leader, or whatever they call them. She'd stand up and say to everyone before the weekly weigh-in, 'Now look, some of you will have put on weight because you ate a whole pizza last night or pigged-out on donuts at the weekend, but guess what? JUST—GET—OVER—IT!' And she's right. By making a conscious decision to rise above our fury with ourselves and others and leave it behind, we're far more likely to fast-track towards a place where contentment is the norm. And I can't believe it's taken me all this time to figure that out.

When I think about that psychotherapist who did nothing but stare at me blankly during approximately a hundred sessions . . . ! Can you think of an easier way to earn big bucks than to just sit with your legs crossed and stare, pretending to listen to the sobbing patient opposite? Would it have killed him to let me into the secret about happiness . . . that it's not so elusive after all. But you know what? I've decided to let go of my anger towards him, because that kind of rage (*any* kind of rage, actually) is non-productive.

> *Feeling wretched for yeas because someone else won't forgive us, well that's just plain stupid.*

Since I started working on this book, I've been revisiting a whole range of situations from the past, seeking out scenarios where I still need to sign off on grievances (perceived or otherwise). And in each case I'm telling myself what Brad's Weight Watchers' lady advised: 'JUST—GET—OVER—IT!'

It's working, which is lovely—and the bonus is that I find I'm looking back on a number of incidents and seeing them through adult eyes for the first time. Here's the perfect example.

Way back . . . A stockbroker I met while skiing asked me to marry him and I said 'Yes!' A couple of months later he changed his mind, deciding to stay with his wife. Yep, the shit was already married, and for a long time afterwards I was furious with him for withdrawing the proposal, staying stuck in an anger I couldn't share with anyone else because it had been a clandestine romance. Today I can see that I could hardly have expected honesty and integrity from a guy who cheated on his wife, and who went on to do so with another woman after me. Furthermore, what was I doing imagining that something good would come from my own involvement in that liaison?

I got what I deserved, but I've now let myself out of the sin-bin, along with the cheat who caused my heartache. I figure I had a lucky escape and, what the hell, it's time to file that one away under 'Lessons I Have Learnt'.

23

DON'T LEAVE YOUR SONG UNSUNG

Most of us are partial to writing down the odd quotation that speaks a truth we need to hear. In my case, I copy the best of them into the front of each year's diary and make it a habit to look at them every morning. One of my all-time best-loved lines is: 'And with a smile you realise that last night's disappointment was merely an experience.' I adore it because it has such a powerful application in situations where I could easily go into revenge-and-hate mode. Instead of allowing bad feelings of resentment to fester, I'm now inspired to put the incident down to being 'an experience'.

Staying stuck in bitterness means it's likely the song you came to sing will remain unsung, and that's incredibly sad.

And as a sort of a bookend to that approach is realising how many of us are super-sensitive, often over-reacting to words and actions that actually weren't meant to cut us to the quick. I got an inkling about this a few years back when I was feeling wounded after a female friend had turned on me. As far as I knew I'd done nothing wrong. I was walking around like some pathetic creature, wondering how anyone could be that mean for no reason. One night at a party I put this to Leon, a man I like very much because he's funny and smart.

'Leon, how would you react if someone did this to you?' He laughed.

'I wouldn't even notice, because I'm so thick-skinned.'

I'm making slow progress, but I'm working on becoming more thick-skinned. When I get there I'll be less likely to take offence and end up in an emotional holding pattern.

I hope it's okay if I share one other quote from the front of my diary, from the Indian poet Tagore: 'Some people spend their lives stringing and unstringing their instrument, while the song they came to sing remains unsung.'

I first copied down that Tagore jewel years ago, and have carried it with me ever since. It goes to the heart of what we're talking about here: letting go of anger and past hurts. The crazy part is that the real truth of it had been staring me in the face all these years, and I missed it until recently. Staying stuck in bitterness means it's likely the song you came to sing will remain unsung, and that's incredibly sad. What a waste.

It's part of the maturing process, I guess, but I'm redefining just what really matters in my life. I'm increasingly drawn to discussions about what it takes to be a decent person, and how we can get there. Space exploration, for example, leaves me totally bored, compared with finding a sparkling quote that is uplifting and inspiring. Mars can die with her secret for all I care—and even if they find streets up there paved with delicious white chocolate, that will never excite me as much as learning a new lesson in the quest for the good life here on earth.

24

WHEN SOMEONE WANTS YOU DEAD

You know how it is when romance is the only thing on your mind and it seems that everywhere you go you're bumping into other couples in love? Kind of the law of attraction, I suppose. Well, here I am, right now, pre-occupied with the endless possibilities of making amends, and I'm constantly unearthing fascinating stories about people at various stages on the road to resolution. And the great thing is, nearly all of them offer life lessons, which is very exciting for a late-starter like *moi*.

The one that has latched on to my heart the most is about a man who forgave his eleven-year-old daughter who consistently wished he was dead, and told him so. The two hadn't seen each other for several years, and when the father was dying of liver cancer he was mindful the girl could well suffer emotionally in the years to come as she thought back on her harsh remarks, and perhaps would feel riddled with guilt that she may have somehow caused his awful death.

In his last weeks of this terminal illness he obtained permission from the family court to leave behind a letter and DVD for her, in which he basically exonerates her for wanting him dead, and conveys his unconditional love.

It sounds as though he was very special to resist being resentful about the child's hateful attitude towards him. While the two remained estranged, surely we must view the dad as a winner because of his generous heart in extraordinarily painful circumstances. Let's hope someone was there to gently hold his hand as he breathed his last.

That good man's magnificent gesture puts me to shame for all the years I'd become angry at the slightest slight, and would often stayed like that for ages just because someone beat me to a parking space at the mall. I've even fantasised about scratching the side of the other person's car just to get my own back.

This is nuts. It shouldn't matter if we have to do an extra lap of the car park; it's not like lurching through a snow storm on foot! And to think I was quite capable of upgrading a pathetic irritation like that into a bad mood lasting all morning, sending vicious vibes to the other driver.

> *It sounds as though he was very special to resist being resentful about the child's hateful attitude towards him.*

25

FAKE IT 'TIL YOU MAKE IT

A while back I heard a joke which changed everything. It goes like this: a woman is driving around and around in a car park, wondering if she'll ever find a vacant spot. She's desperate, so she says to God: 'Please God, just find me a space and I promise I'll begin going to church again.' Two seconds later there it is, an empty space, right alongside the entrance to the mall. Quick as a flash she says: 'Don't worry God. I found one myself.'

Okay, so the joke has nothing to do with forgiveness, but it really made me laugh. I think of it every time I'm tempted to yell, 'I hope you get a flat tyre today!' to a driver who cruises into a space, fair and square, beating me by a second. *Now* I say to myself, 'Get a grip!' instead of plotting retaliation.

I have to say that Jennifer Aniston is my pin-up girl in these matters. I find her grace under pressure very classy—the way she remained dignified when Brad left her for Angelina in the most public of ways. Hopefully Jen's calm demeanour (despite, no doubt, feeling gutted inside) has allowed her to move on and let bygones be bygones. She certainly deserves to be happy.

The truth is that when you don't spend your time slagging off at each other in these circumstances, everyone can get on with their lives, even if it's really hard to start with. Kylie Minogue was let down big-time by her French hunk boyfriend, Olivier Martinez, but he was there for her during her cancer treatment, and they obviously had some good times. Now they're clearly friends, and it's hard to image that would be possible if Kylie had gone public at the time about her hurt and disappointment. She has the sweet face of someone who knows how to forgive.

> *We all have a choice as to whether we forgive or not.*

Meanwhile, Britney Spears has had some real demons to face, but she's back out in public, and surely deserves another chance. There must have been some tough moments of self-forgiveness in order for her to do that. And on the road back, there must also be plenty of times when she needs to fake confidence and joy. I for one wish her all the very best.

But don't get me started on how my vicious side used to come out when the same two women up the back began chatting, as usual, during Pilates. It spoilt the experience completely. I always felt like marching over and hitting them, quite sure in that moment I'd hate the two of them for at least another twenty years. Mind you, I'm now a lot better than I was. Here's my effective technique: I look over at the one doing the most chattering and say under my breath: 'I bless the sister.'

Trust me . . . it works, but you have to fake it 'til you make it.

26

DON'T SWEAT THE SMALL STUFF

Here's another real doozy from my sorry scrapbook: around fifteen years ago I was at the home of a male friend I adore who had just returned from a trip to Europe. He disappeared into the bedroom and returned with an exquisite silk scarf he'd bought for someone else in Paris.

'I can't give it to her because it's stained; my aftershave leaked on it in the suitcase. Would *you* like it?'

Bad enough he was offering me damaged goods that he wouldn't dream of giving some other woman—worse, I accepted!! 'Thank you', I said, and took the damn scarf with a big stain on it . . . then I seethed for years, angry with him for treating me as a second-class citizen.

I'm over that now because I happened upon Eleanor Roosevelt's astute comment: 'No one can make you feel inferior without your permission.'

I look back on the litany of petty offences that have managed to bug me and I'm sick with shame. Gee, which would be tougher: having someone speak while you're exercising, or knowing your eleven-year-old daughter genuinely wants you dead?

That poor father. I wonder if he knows he died a hero? He's certainly one of *my* heroes. It's to be hoped his daughter one day gets to see the DVD he left behind and is inspired to be kind in all her relationships.

For me, the take-home message from this tale of almost Greek-tragedy proportions is that if we remain unforgiving for a long, long time, death might scoop up our adversary and we'll wake up and realise that ship has sailed. The chance to mend fences will have gone forever.

I was at a birthday party not long after reading about that hapless father and his daughter, and I shared the details with another guest, Ruth, who I was meeting for the first time. She told me that both her parents had been in concentration camps. This led to a discussion between us about how deep one has to dig to find the inner beauty that allows for forgiveness in the aftermath of such great suffering.

Ruth went on to talk about a documentary that had deeply moved her, featuring a woman who'd been in a World War II death camp during her teen years. It came out that the worst of many shocking experiences in that camp that befell this poor woman happened when she was talking to her sister. The next moment a guard comes up to them and shoots her sister dead, right in front of her. It's hard to imagine the depth of her revulsion, powerlessness, and overwhelming sense of loss. Sisters are meant to look after each other, but what could this woman do?

She spent the next fifty or so years paralysed with terrible grief and resentment, until she decided the only way forward was to be whole again. Even though she was now an elderly woman she decided to try and find the commandant of that camp, confront him, then make peace. She located him and, against the odds, they become quite close. According to Ruth, there's an extraordinary scene in the documentary where the two of them are walking along, holding hands, as the friends they have become.

No-one can make us feel inferior without our permission.

We all have a choice as to whether we forgive or not. If this brave woman was able to do it with a hurt so unspeakable, then so can we with our everyday annoyances and let-downs. And nothing is more annoying in an everyday kind of way than finding out the object of your affections is a love rat.

I come back to this theme over and over because it's the 'Will I or won't I forgive' scenario we can all identify with. You can't shoot 'em, but forgiving seems like a bit of a stretch in the immediate aftermath of finding out you've been played for a fool.

I recall like it was yesterday being taken aside at a party, out of the hearing of my boyfriend. The hostess worked in a flower shop and she thought I should know my prince had been in the day before to place an order for red roses. She knows I'm not a fan of red roses, so she discreetly paid attention as her colleague attended to this customer. After he walked out, she managed a quick glance at the handwritten card he'd left to go with the roses. And what a romantic note it was too. Only problem was, it wasn't headed my way.

I thanked the hostess for giving me the low-down, and then I marched over to my boyfriend out on the terrace and demanded to know what he was up to. Yes, he was seeing someone else on the side. I ended our relationship there and then, spending the next couple of years being angry with him *and* with the messenger who'd spilled the beans.

I now had *two* people to forgive, and it wasn't easy. Not for the first time, I was left wondering whether it would have been better had I not found out.

Don't get me started. I've got a stack of these stories, all with me as the patsy. I need to know: is it just me, or does this stuff happen to other people too?

27

FORGIVENESS POSTER BOYS

Of course the universal pin-up boy in the forgiveness stakes is Nelson Mandela, whose grace during and after decades of captivity just takes your breath away. He didn't hate then, and still doesn't.

I once met Kathy Sledge from the iconic pop group Sister Sledge, best-loved for the unforgettable chart-topper 'We Are Family'. She told me that when she met Nelson Mandela he hugged her and said that when he was in prison he could hear the guards' radio, and what kept him going was 'We Are Family' playing from time to time. It sustained him to know he was part of the wider human family.

Up there with Mandela is the Dalai Lama, who has also known deprivation on a giant scale. The Tibetan spiritual leader was forced to flee his country for India in 1959 when China cracked down on dissidents, nine years after its People's Liberation Army had invaded Tibet. That's exactly fifty years as a displaced person, yet the Dalai Lama is always smiling. Part of his secret seems to be that he doesn't hold grudges. That's certainly the impression he gives in all his public speaking. I have a theory: he finds joy in the *small* things, and this helps take his mind off the big worries which would threaten to torment and destroy a lesser person.

> *It sustained him to know he was part of the wider human family.*

I have a little story about him which illustrates this. One of former British Prime Minister Sir Edward Heath's most charming anecdotes was about his friendship with the Dalai Lama. When Heath was going to Tibet on one occasion he rang the spiritual leader in exile, asking if there was anything he could do for him whilst in Tibet. The then PM expected to be asked to carry out some serious task but, no, the Dali Lama simply asked Sir Edward to go and check on his prized jazz record collection, left behind when he fled his country.

Presumably the Dali Lama's optimistic nature allows him to imagine that he will one day return to his beloved Tibet, where he will once more be able to enjoy the simple pleasure of playing his records.

28

GREAT SUFFERING, FOLLOWED BY FORGIVENESS

My own five cents worth is that God was showing off when He created Phan Thi Kim Phuc, who suffered horribly during the Vietnam War. Everyone will know the famous photograph of her as a naked nine year old running towards a camera, her clothes shed because they had been set alight with napalm, which had been dropped on her village as the consequence of an order from a US commander. It was June 1972. When the picture went round the world, it became a turning point in that shocking war.

Today she travels to many countries, campaigning for peace, never shying away from acknowledging that iconic photograph; in fact she wants to see it exposed to future generations: 'Let the world see how terrible war can be.'

On another occasion I read that she said, 'We have to move on to help each other [and] I wanted to forgive the people who caused my suffering. I did—and so I am free from hatred and bitterness.'

Whenever I read about her selfless work, I think of how she suffered such overwhelming pain and despair, as her life literally went up in flames. I'm left wondering how she has managed to let go of her rage.

Not many men get to be a hero twice in one lifetime.

In the context of the Vietnam War, it would be remiss not to make mention of the extreme suffering of John McCain during his years being held captive, and tortured, by the North Vietnamese—and of his eventual expedition from hate to forgiveness. Who would blame him if he went to Hanoi armed with a semi-automatic weapon and the home addresses of his tormentors? And certainly the hate stayed in his heart for some years.

But on CNN in recent times I heard him say, 'I think the point is that I believe in redemption. I believe in forgiveness. And I forgave my North Vietnamese captors, who didn't treat me very well. I forgave the anti-war movement and reconciled with them. My life has been spent in reconciliation and redemption and that's why I believe in redemption.'

Not many men get to be a hero twice in one lifetime.

29

LOSING AT LOVE, AND STILL COMING OUT A WINNER

Losing at Love, and Still Coming Out a Winner

It never ceases to amaze me how heartless some people can be, especially when they're close to us and act shabbily, such as serious betrayal. They don't even realise their behaviour is reprehensible! They should not be surprised to find out that others are having trouble letting go of resentment towards them . . . but they *would* be because they're too self-absorbed to get the message they've done anything wrong. I have permission to share the following story, and I do so because it offers an insight into a way to triumph over treachery.

Years ago Amy meets Edward, a lovely man a little older than her, and they launch into a romance. One night, when she has a date planned with her beau, she takes ill and her sister, Elizabeth, goes in her place so as not to stand Edward up. Elizabeth, continues to go out with Edward and, because of the social mores of the time, he feels that as Elizabeth is the elder of two single daughters he should marry *her*. They then ask Amy to be bridesmaid at the wedding that should have been hers.

The newly-weds move to another state and have their first baby. When a second child is almost due, Edward has to take a job that means he won't be home very often, so he asks Amy if she will uproot her life and relocate to live with them in order to help Elizabeth take care of the children! Amy and their widowed mother both move to the other state to assist Elizabeth with the kids. Amy later meets a wonderful man, and they marry, have two children, and share a truly fulfilling and successful marriage . . . until he dies at 68.

During their married lives, both families remain living near each other, sharing Christmases and birthdays, with the earlier disloyalty towards Amy never mentioned until . . .

Years later when Edward is in his early eighties, he sadly gets dementia and is eventually moved into care. One day when Amy is visiting with her younger daughter, Edward makes it clear he hates being in a dementia ward, and asks them to grab a newspaper and help him find an apartment to move into, adding that he doesn't want to go back to Elizabeth. He turns to Amy and says, 'I should have married you in the first place all those years ago.'

. . . the following story . . . offers an insight into a way to triumph over treachery.

Amy's daughter reckons Edward's admission 'probably gave Mum the ability to let the hurt go. It was a wonderful moment for her, and for me too.'

I assure you Amy does not have a mean bone in her body but—back to my assertion that happiness is the best revenge—Amy's match made in heaven with her husband who died too young was the perfect way to say 'Up yours' to Edward and Elizabeth (even though such a crass idea would never have occurred to this fine lady).

30

WHEN LOVES GOES BAD—GET OVER IT!

It's a whole different ball game when it's relatives who shaft us, because it seems to be against nature. But when push comes to shove, blood can prove to be as thin as water, while a marriage certificate may count for nothing either when lust or greed prove irresistible. It's dismaying just how often the most heartfelt wedding vows disintegrate, with nothing left to show for the union but treachery and acrimony.

Whenever I contemplate this sad scenario in its many manifestations, I usually spare a thought for Walter, an older man I used to know, and actually dated a couple of times. His wife had left him for someone else twenty years earlier, and he remained furious and deeply upset. It was his *raison d'être* to actively loathe her and say terrible things about her to anyone who would listen. His unwillingness to move on was pathetic to witness, especially when I heard stories of the ex-wife's dreamy life with husband number two. She possibly never gave her ex a second's thought.

I suspect he imagined that, by hating her, he was somehow punishing her. He got that wrong.

Once we went to the opening night of a play. It was a revival of a 1930s farce—light and silly; definitely not to be taken seriously. But my companion was fuming all evening. As we walked out to get a taxi he was complaining about the play, which was about a woman who left her husband.

'Lighten up', I said. 'It was a *comedy*.'

'You could have fooled me', replied Walter through gritted teeth.

> *I guess he imagined that, by hating her, he was somehow punishing her. He got that wrong.*

He has really only marked time during the second half of his life, whereas happiness would have been a much smarter form of revenge. He just didn't understand that throwing the ashes of his marriage off a cliff and starting over would have meant giving himself the ultimate gift.

While I probably sound short-tempered with this character, I really do find it such a pity the way he aches for what he can no longer have. At some level he believed his quota of fulfilment was used up when his wife left him. As though joy is a finite thing.

I once shared with him a sentiment expressed by the great pianist Artur Rubenstein, but it didn't go over too well. Rubenstein had said:

I live by one principle: enjoy life with no conditions! People say, 'If I had your health, if I had your money, oh, I would enjoy myself'. It is not true. I would be happy if I were lying sick in a hospital bed. It must come from the inside. This is one thing I hope I have contributed to my children, by examples and talk: to understand that life is a wonderful thing and to enjoy it, every day, to the full.

This quote went straight over Walter's head, cutting no ice with him. The last time I bumped into him he was just the same. He did, however, share an amusing account of having seen the ex-wife at a party, their first encounter in twenty years.

'I was at a gallery opening and this woman of a certain age who looked like Barbara Bush came up and asked me if I'd like a drink. I replied, "That's terribly nice of you", and when she returned with my wine, I almost fainted when she said: "Well, we certainly have much to be proud of with our children, don't we?" It was my ex-wife, looking about eighty. I didn't even recognise her!'

She wasn't any longer the sexy brunette he couldn't get out of his mind, and I told Walter that this was a sign he should forget her and what happened between them all those years ago. But, no, he didn't. Decades of anger had done him in and he indicated he fully intended keeping on with the vindictive thoughts.

I gave up. The last thing I said to him that day was, 'Walter, knock yourself out'.

What his life became is pathetic in several ways. One is that he has an ever-diminishing assortment of acquaintances willing to stand still and listen to his vitriolic comments about the ex-wife. This verbal vomit tumbles out his mouth at parties, and it makes people move away. He doesn't realise he's turned into a loathsome bore. Or maybe he knows and he just doesn't care any more.

Part Four

FORGIVING
YOURSELF

31

FORGIVING YOURSELF...
THAT'S THE TOUGH ONE

I have lately become a bit of a magnet for tales of betrayal—only some of which end in reconciliation, and I'm grateful for all the personal experiences I've been entrusted with. I can say without any doubt that what happened to Rebecca touched me even more than any of the others I'd been told.

Based in California, Rebecca has a great job in television programming, but at night she goes home alone to the apartment she once shared with the love of her life, Jason, whom she cared for during years of serious illness. Today, five years after Jason's death, Rebecca still has what she refers to as her 'dilemma re forgiveness: do I or don't I?'

When Jason first needed a kidney transplant, three of his siblings were tested—two brothers and one sister—with another sister not having volunteered. His sister who tested was the only one of the volunteers who was compatible, but was not an ideal candidate.

Anyone who has been down the transplant roller-coaster will know what it felt like for this family when there were medical complications regarding the sister's suitability. Rebecca told me:

> She had very high blood pressure and the specialist disqualified her from becoming a donor. You can imagine how awful that was. She, however, insisted and persisted, until they finally gave in. I might add that she almost died on the operating table from severe haemorrhaging. I will always be eternally grateful to her because she gave him almost thirteen years of quality life.

Later Jason became very ill again and the doctors said he had an infection and was in all likelihood going to lose the kidney. Over the next couple of months it was just a matter of time, and once again Rebecca set about finding a donor for her soul mate.

After all is said and done, I think the person I find hardest to forgive throughout all of this, is myself.

The second sister who had not been tested for the first transplant was really the only other sibling who could potentially help, but as Rebecca sensed this woman was hoping not to be asked, Rebecca put her own hand up to be the next donor for Jason.

> After going through all the tests, I was compatible, albeit not a perfect match, but enough to proceed with the transplant.

The operation was scheduled, but the months leading up to it were difficult for Jason. He was not at all happy about my having what he considered unnecessary major surgery. When the time came he was desperately ill and I couldn't wait for the whole thing to be over and have my big strong Jason back.

The operation was seemingly a success and he was up and about before I was. He was the star patient at the hospital and they just loved him! Unfortunately, because I was not a particularly good match, he was put on experimental anti-rejection drugs that didn't agree with him, so the next few months became arduous. Fourteen months later he was diagnosed with colon cancer and doctors removed all but six inches of his colon, his right adrenal gland, his spleen and a couple of tumors . . . a lengthy operation that seemed like it was never going to end. Twelve hours it took.

From somewhere Rebecca found the strength to press on, but this loving couple received another blow a couple of days later when Jason had a heart attack and required three stents. Fortunately, throughout all of this the kidney held up relatively well, which was amazing.

After almost a month in hospital he came home, only to be rushed back in with a major haemorrhage. Jason couldn't seem to get an even break, and this was compounded by the new kidney eventually experiencing chronic rejection. It was now only a matter of time.

'Once again we were devastated. Jason always told me that if he ever had to have dialysis it would be the end for him—and, alas, that turned out to be true,' said Rebecca. Still holding down her high-powered job, she took Jason to dialysis three times a week, and always picked him up.

'It was such a trial just to get him in and out of the facility. He needed a wheelchair to get him to and from the car and he was a big man—six foot, five inches, and I am five foot, four inches. Walking into that place was a nightmare for me, and to see him sitting there so lost and alone is something that will haunt me until the day I die.'

Rebecca saw no shame in begging, so she went back to the best person now available to become a donor, his second sister who had been somewhat reluctant the first times around.

She said 'Yes', but after discussing it with her husband and her doctor she was again coming up with all sorts of excuses and Jason sensed that she just wasn't comfortable with it, so he decided to nip it in the bud. He told Rebecca he detected such relief in the sister's voice when he said to her that his doctor thought she was probably too old to be a donor. Rebecca told me:

In my desperation I wrote to his niece in Florida—she was 28 and unmarried. It was her mother who had been the first donor, so I was hopeful she'd be a good match. I poured my heart out and I wasn't too proud to beg! I didn't hear from her for a long time and eventually she called and said she had misplaced the letter. That was a red herring for me because I wondered how something so important could be something she would just set aside and lose! Anyway, she said she'd be willing to be tested, but I didn't hear anymore from her and felt I couldn't push too hard.

Then Jason was diagnosed with lung cancer. His lung was removed and this, combined with the need for regular dialysis, meant he was becoming weaker and weaker, and the family was aware of his condition. One of his brothers, who would have willingly given him a kidney but was not compatible, came from New York to visit, along with Jason's second sister and the niece from Florida. They were shocked to see how much he had deteriorated.

Both Jason and Rebecca held out hope that the niece would mention she wanted to donate her kidney—but she never did. Rebecca told me that to this day she believes that was the point her once-strong husband really gave up. He knew he wouldn't survive another five to six years waiting for a cadaver donor, and he died in his sleep a month later.

So ... that is where I have difficulty with forgiveness. Not that either his sister, who didn't volunteer, or his niece didn't love him. They most definitely did, of that I have no doubt. I have to consider that maybe fear was a factor. But ... this was my husband, it was *my* life as well as his because he was all that I had in this world, and I was losing him. When I thought that maybe, just maybe, one of them could have saved his life. When you're about to lose the one person you love more than anything, you think the whole world should stand up and say, 'Me ... me ... take my kidney, or whatever you need!'

Through the tears, Rebecca explained that, in the five years since Jason's death, she has tried to come to terms with all of this; sometimes feeling she has totally forgiven, while other times she still asks herself, 'Why didn't they help us?' Then she reminds herself that they had families too, 'and what if something happened to someone in *their* life and they were then unable to help. But all of that really makes no difference to me. This was my world, my husband, and nothing else really matters.'

She made it very clear that she goes on loving Jason's family very much, but that way deep down she'll always wonder why more of his close relatives didn't step up to the plate. If they had, maybe he'd still be with her—or at least that's how she sees it.

Her grief is still so intense that I almost felt I could reach out and touch it. I just wished there was a way I could take some of her pain away, but it remains too raw to be eased by just a soothing word. She aches for her loss, and laments that others who could have helped, didn't. And to add to her torture, Rebecca comes down hard on herself too:

After all is said and done, I think the person I find hardest to forgive throughout all of this, is myself. There must have been something else I could have done that I didn't. I don't quite know what, but for the rest of my life I think I'll always be searching for some sign from somewhere that tells me I did the best I could under the circumstances.

So forgiveness for myself or others involved—I don't know that it will ever really happen because there will always be that little bit of resentment. So, is there some such thing as semi-forgiveness . . . guess not, huh? You either do or you don't.

I'm convinced Rebecca doesn't have the faintest idea how remarkable she is. Her efforts to keep Jason alive were quite simply super-human, and I pray she finds a way to smile again.

32

WHEN FAMILY LIFE IS A BATTLEFIELD

A couple of months ago, I went with a friend, Jennie, to see a medium who came highly recommended, and she did not disappoint. Over the years, Jennie and I had made double appointments with a motley array of soothsayers and clairvoyants (is it just me, or have you noticed that these people always have yappy little dogs that have seen better days?). Quite frankly, most of the time the readings were not worth leaving home for. My other complaint is that fortune tellers never, ever live anywhere handy. You have to drive for ages to get to them. Why is that?

So we go to see Lesley, way out at a beachside suburb. After the session we are in agreement that this pleasant woman is indeed a genuine medium . . . and not a yappy dog in sight. So when Jennie goes back to her place she immediately rings an old mate, Stuart, who is facing professional challenges of his own at the time in Boston, where he works as an architect. He is due to arrive that weekend to stay with Jennie and her husband for a short break from his stresses. She tells him, 'When you're here you've got to go and see Lesley, this amazing medium. I'll make an appointment for you.' She has a feeling that this was something he *must* do.

At that point Stuart was only a name to me, someone Jennie and her husband spoke of warmly. Little did I know that I would later meet Stuart and hear first-hand about a life of hate that had defined him, but which was turned around into forgiveness during just one session with Lesley, the medium.

'Forgiveness happens at a couple of levels'.

Several weeks later, after hearing from Jennie about the book I was writing, Stuart offered to meet up with me, and I leapt at the opportunity. He arrived smiling, with the look of a man finally on the right path.

'On the way here today I thought, Gee, I feel good about this—and the reason I'm doing this is that I actually think the story I'm about to give to you is also part of the journey and meant to be—and part of the closure, in the hope you'll share it with other people. If you and Jennie hadn't gone to the medium and then she hadn't told me about it, I probably wouldn't have taken the step I have.' What started to unfold was Stuart's ugly relationship with his father when he was growing up—and this was at the heart of what he needed to forgive.

His brother, Keith, was six years older and his sister, Sylvia, sixteen months younger. His earliest memory is of being five, and his mother being hit by his father, who was an alcoholic. He was always drunk and constantly smoked—he'd have three or four cigarettes even before he'd get out of bed in the morning.

And many times they didn't have food on the table because their father would go up to the golf club and put all the money into poker machines. He changed his job quite a bit—worked in a bank, moved around and then ran a couple of petrol stations.

He also used to hit Keith, who ran away from home a few times because he couldn't handle the violence. He mostly hit Keith and the mother, but, when she was older, Sylvia too. Never Stuart though, which he always found strange. I felt physically sick, though, when Stuart added, 'The fact that he didn't ever hit me wasn't any sort of relief, because there was enough violence around me that I felt the hurt of that. You don't need to be physically hit to feel the violence.' Equally disturbing to hear was Stuart's account of something his old man did one night when he was drunk.

'He didn't know where he was and he got out of bed to go to the bathroom and came into my room and peed on me, thinking he was standing in front of toilet.' I conveyed my horror to Stuart, but he didn't allow me to offer sympathy for the indignity of that night. He made it clear he didn't need anyone feeling sorry for him. He simply wanted to keep rolling out the story that had been bottled up for so long.

When he had the petrol stations I'd go and do casual work there as a small boy and at times he'd take off down to the pub and I'd be running the petrol station (with the mechanic watching over me) and he'd come back, loaded to the eyeballs, and there were a number of occasions he'd sit me in the car on his lap: he'd change the gears and I'd steer, because he couldn't see—he was so out of it. That was an interesting way of learning how to drive.

There are certain things you actually blank out of your memory—because you don't want to go there.

He revealed that his mother said to the children on a number of occasions, 'We're outta here', when the mistreatment became too much, and she'd take them to stay at an aunt's place—or they'd just roam around for a while, eventually returning home.

This dreadful man who fell short as a husband and father was committed to a psychiatric hospital and had electro-shock therapy, which didn't work by the way.

Part of the reason he was put in there is that on a number of occasions he threatened to commit suicide. In front of us, standing there with a knife. So there was a lot of strange behaviour, plus he was having an affair. He didn't beat Mum and Sylvia and Keith so bad that they were hospitalised, but it was mental abuse as well. Torment all the time.

Often he'd close the garage down and we'd head off to the pub early and he'd sit me in the car and go and get me a whole lot of jelly beans. I'd ask, 'Why can't I walk home? It's only up the hill', and he'd say, 'No, you wait there'. I'd be there for two hours by myself, which I guess helps explain why I like my own company.

He'd play golf often and I'd caddy for him and then I'd have to sit in the car while he was inside blowing the week's takings on the poker machines. He'd finally come out unable to walk straight, and then we'd go home and he'd have no money left.

Stuart's old man was committed to an insane ward at a veterans' hospital but that was unsuccessful, as things turned out. One day, soon after he returned home, he suddenly announced to Sylvia, Stuart, Keith, their mother and Keith's teenage girlfriend, who was pregnant, 'You're all outta here now. Just get out.' And he physically picked up Sylvia and threw her out, then one by one ejected the others, until Stuart's stunned family was in the front yard, and then the father slammed the door.

That was it. It was the last I ever saw of my father. His mistress promptly moved in and took up residence. We had no clothes, nothing, zero. So what happened, my uncle and aunty had recently moved to the city near us, and we stayed with them for a bit, and my uncle went down and got some clothes for us from our house, but that was it. Next Sylvia and I were shunted off to live with various relatives in the country until mum could get a job, which she did, packing fruit.

Then we came back to live in rented accommodation—just two rooms with a kitchenette in the corner. Mum and Sylvia shared a bed and I slept on a banana lounge. I did a paper run, and after two more moves I finally got my own bed!

I asked Stuart if, despite the financial hardship, life was easier without the abuse?

Yes, no doubt about that, but the importance of family support cannot be underestimated either. Mum was one of eleven girls and the support that came around us was remarkable and it was what got us through.

The concept of hate changes as you get older and you understand the reality of the depth of what took place. The feelings of hate towards him definitely intensified as I got older. I never saw Dad again and never wanted to. When I was fifteen, the hate started to kick in big-time. I'd think, 'I don't have a father . . . yes I do, but he's a prick.' The hate does intensify. I got to the point where I openly said, 'If I ever saw him on the street, I'd fucking kill the prick for what he did to us.' Any time his name came up at home I'd say, 'I want to kill the bastard'—such was the depth of my loathing.

Fortunately in my gallivanting days in my late twenties, I met my wife, Angela, and when we decided to get married I thought long and hard about what this meant, given what happened with my father, and I decided to change my name. I said to Angela, 'I hate him so much that this is an opportunity to cut a cord. It's about a new beginning.' I didn't want my wife or my children to carry his name. That's how deeply I felt about it. This was very important to me.

Why does the hate increase with the years? I don't have an answer to that.

I had learnt from Jennie that Stuart and Angela have a very happy marriage and are loving parents to their two teenage children. I asked Stuart how he managed to be such a caring family man, given the abuse in the home in which he grew up.

Largely because of the example my mother set me, as did her sisters and their families.

For a long time now Angela has been saying to me: 'Stuart, you need to let this go. It's not good to have this depth of hatred in your being; it's negative.' And whenever she raised this I'd say, 'Angie, he was a bastard and I'll never ever forget what he did to us, and I'll never forgive'.

My sister, Sylvia, for the last ten years has been saying the same thing. She had finally let go herself, after great traumas in her mature life. The fact she has survived what she survived and forgiven our father is truly remarkable.

The inability to forgive increased for me as I got older and then it levelled out. It's something that's always with you. It never went away, and every time I thought of it I got very upset.

Stuart's mother died fifteen years ago from a massive brain haemorrhage and, according to Stuart, she continued hating his father right to the end. He added, 'But they must have loved each other at some point . . . and I do remember my father being the life of the party, so I suppose he was easy to love in the early days.'

Stuart spoke frankly about the on-going demons in his family. His daughter, Jackie, has been going through major depression issues for the past ten years, his sister has tried to kill herself, and sadly her son did commit suicide, and all this is now understood as linked with their father's inherited mental illness.

Forgiveness happens at a number of levels, but we're talking here of a personal forgiveness, and as a result of what has happened to me recently, I've been through a journey as a consequence . . . but there are other areas of my thought process and view on life where I find it very difficult to forgive other people, and what has occurred. I think 'You bastards!' even though it's got nothing to do with me—and paedophilia is one example of that, along with what is going on in Iraq: the murder of one million people on a lie! Should I, for example, forgive Bush? So far I can't.

Stuart had never been to someone like Lesley and he didn't know what to expect. He told her nothing about himself, but as soon as he sat down, she said, 'Your mother and father are here and both of them are saying they love you and how proud they are of you—although your father is more in the background, looking a bit sheepish. Your mother is saying that she and your father are together and that they love each other.'

Next Lesley is asking him, 'You had a difficult childhood and you didn't like your father, did you?' Stuart said, 'Yes'. She went on: 'Your mum is reinforcing that they're in love, and your dad is saying it wasn't his fault—that he had a condition he inherited from his father, and that he's sorry for what happened, but it was his physical manifestation, not the spiritual.'

'Your Mum is saying that you need to forgive your father because you need to move on and she's saying you must understand that she and your father are in love. She wants you to forgive him.'

Stuart is telling me of these extraordinary events in a calm and measured way.

I explain to Lesley I'm on a spiritual journey and that I don't know where to go next; I had hit a road block and did not know what to do about it. At that point in the reading I felt a pressure on my head and my temperature rose and I was short of breath. I felt a peace and I felt loved, and I described the sensation to Lesley, who said, 'Yes, your spirit guide is standing behind you'. She introduced him to me and I was told he had been with me all my life. She added, 'Your guide says you need to forgive your father'. She said that I must write a forgiveness note, then burn it, and by doing that I'll be able to move forward with my spiritual journey.

I knew in that moment that this was the truth, and I felt at complete peace.

When I got home I thought about the whole thing and I told Angela and the kids, because they knew about my journey. I'd been told to forgive my father and I'm sitting there for two or three weeks thinking, 'Jesus, I've got to forgive this prick for me to go down that spiritual path'. I worked out that the process had to include not just forgiveness, but meaning, forethought and honesty. I couldn't do it without any accountability.

I did a letter in pencil, then another in ink and I went outside and burnt them, and watched the ashes, and then let the wind take them away over the next few days. I don't wish to discuss in detail what I said to my father in that letter, other than to say I acknowledged that the physical manifestation was out of his control.

I asked Stuart to sum up the difference in how he feels now.

'I think I'm still coming to terms with it, but I'm very glad I did it. I feel so happy, I feel as if a weight has been lifted off my soul. An important part of this was telling my sister I had forgiven our father. She smiled, "I knew you would". I asked how she knew and she said, "I've been praying for you to do this for many years, and the prayer group I'm in has been praying for you too".'

As we were winding up, I spontaneously reached out and shook Stuart's hand, simply saying, 'Congratulations'. Then asked one last question: 'Do you now feel sad that you spent so long hating?'

I don't think I've had enough time to reflect on that but to the extent we are all the sum total of what we've been through, I don't know what sort of person I would have become without that baggage—and I have to say that I have a successful life, and I'm happy, and I have a loving family.

You're asking if I feel regret? Well in the context of how I feel today, as against how I felt before—unquestionably. This is a fabulous feeling now.

33

TAKE A CHANCE: STEP OUTSIDE YOUR COMFORT ZONE

Deep down, I suspect part of why I'm now so drawn to the Stuarts of this world is that I'm hoping some of their goodness will rub off. You see, I fully get it that I don't deserve a medal for silently absolving the chatterers in my Pilates class. This is kindergarten stuff compared with what many people have been through.

And as I think through the lessons to be found in the stories I've been privileged to examine, a recurring theme seems to be that there was a pivotal point for most of them when they finally chose LIFE. A decision was made to forgive others their transgressions, and without exception this has allowed them to break through the clouds and see the sun.

I have a theory: each time we let go of the rage associated with someone else's *minor* misdemeanours towards us, we inch closer to being in a head space where true forgiveness is possible, however great the hurt. So creating the habit of *not* stringing out our wrath in response to small acts of disloyalty sets us up to deal in a mature way with serious treachery and malice, when these things come along.

> *A recurring theme seems to be that there was a pivotal point for most of them when they finally chose LIFE.*

I will never forget the joy on the faces of Adrianna and Stuart as they described the freedom, and sense of all things being possible, once they decided to let go of their lingering pain from the past and look only to the future.

There's a chance, however, that a forgiveness-watcher like me might be in danger of imagining I'm becoming a better person by osmosis—purely by meeting or reading about others who have done something brave to resolve bitterness—with me not bothering to step outside my *own* comfort zone to any great extent. I do the same thing with dieting: I devour diets published in magazines, and I never miss TV programs about obese people losing half their body weight, as though my passive observations will somehow render me thinner and fitter.

Others can inspire us, but then we need to get off the couch and take a few risks of our own for that inspiration to mean anything other than entertainment value . . . but sometimes the story being told is so immense that we stay firmly on the couch, unavailable to visualise ourselves carrying off such heroism.

34

WOMAN IN A MILLION

This chapter heading was my initial response when I first heard about Ingrid Betancourt's rescue, following four years of captivity in the Columbian jungle. She was running for president in that country, when she insisted on visiting the former demilitarised zone by military aircraft. President Pastrana and his aides turned down this demand, arguing that not even the Columbian Army could guarantee her well-being during the turmoil that would follow the retaking of the DMZ. So she decided to go there by road with a couple of political aides.

She was stopped at the last military checkpoint, and officers insisted her group not proceed to San Vicente del Caguan, the village being used for the peace talks. Betancourt dismissed their warnings and continued her journey. When she reached a checkpoint manned by FARC (the rebel organisation), she was captured and spent much of the next six years tied to a tree in the jungle, never seeing sunlight, due to the thick foliage overhead.

Finally four of her fellow hostages (former politicians) were freed. They went public about their concern for the health of Ingrid Betancourt, with one describing her as 'exhausted physically and in her morale'. They went on to describe how she was mistreated very badly: 'They have vented their anger on her, they have her chained up in inhumane conditions.' Another said that she had Hepatitis B and was near death.

> *What can one say about a heart capable of such infinite love and forgiveness?*

The day her family had long prayed for arrived five months later, when Betancourt and three American hostages were recovered. Betancourt did not shy away from questions posed by the world's media, and she alluded to being tortured during her captivity.

The freed hostages indicated they had spent much of their time in captivity saying the rosary. Betancourt was quoted as telling journalists, 'I am convinced this is a miracle of the Virgin Mary. To me it is clear she has had a hand in all of this'; then only a couple of weeks after being freed she and her family made a pilgrimage to Lourdes to give thanks, and to pray for her captors and for those who remained hostage.

I repeat: she *prayed* for her captors—after they had tortured her for six years! What can one say about a heart capable of such infinite love and forgiveness?

Then only days later, on Colombia's Independence Day, Ingrid Betancourt reached out with a powerful message to the FARC, her tormentors for all those years, urging their leaders to stop the bloodshed.

'It is time to drop those weapons and change them for roses, substitute them with tolerance, respect, and as brothers that we are, find a way so that we can all live together in the world, live together in Colombia.'

Curiously, it was just a day after Betancourt's plea for peace to the Columbian rebels, that I noticed a tiny item in a newspaper with a plea for forgiveness from the East Timorese President, Jose Ramos-Horta, calling on the East Timorese to accept that the Indonesians who committed human rights abuses against them would never be tried.

Indonesia is not exactly famous for saying 'sorry' for its human rights abuses, and given Indonesia's might as a nation, a little dot on the map like East Timor is in no position to demand an apology. I mention these stories because for all of us, forgiveness is obviously harder when the offender has no interest in making amends.

35

LIFE BEYOND REVENGE

It's so hard to contemplate the additional challenge associated with letting go of resentment when the person who harmed you doesn't look like apologising, ever. Perhaps even more tormenting is when we just don't understand why they did what they did.

> *Then the day came when, as he put it, 'When I decided I no longer wanted to live in a stage of revenge.'*

It definitely takes an amazing human being to let go of a need for explanations, and to forgive anyway. This is only a guess, because I'm far from being this evolved myself, but that sounds like the place where the bus leaves for enlightenment.

No amount of longing and regret will ever change a set of circumstances, and accepting that life doesn't always work out the way we would like is a jumping-off point for good times—such as new beginnings.

I'm a huge fan of Dominick Dunne, who fills a part of me that no other writer can. Widely regarded as being at his best when writing on true crime, never has he been more touching than when he wrote about the murder of his actress daughter, Dominique.

After an abusive affair with Los Angeles chef, John Sweeney, Dominique ended the relationship; then, just a few weeks later, Sweeney strangled Dominique in the driveway of her home after she refused to get back with him. She died a few days later in hospital, aged just 22.

Sweeney was convicted of manslaughter and sentenced to six and a half years in prison. He served less than four years before his release, having been given credit for time served before conviction.

Only a month ago I saw a repeat on cable of a documentary about Mr Dunne, in which he spoke frankly about the dark years after his daughter's murder. He was in so much pain he longed to see the killer suffer, and even contemplated ways to harm him. Then the day came when, as he put it, 'I decided I no longer wanted to live in a state of revenge.'

How exquisite is that? I guess that was the day he freed himself up to make a new beginning.

36

CONDITIONAL FORGIVENESS

The Dunne case reminded me of Garry Lynch, another remarkable man, who lost his twenty-six-year-old daughter to violence, and he too discovered how to move away from 'a state of revenge', although he stopped short of holding out a hand of friendship to the bastards who raped, tortured and murdered his beautiful daughter, Anita Cobby.

I covered part of the lengthy trial in which the five scumbags were convicted for their truly unspeakable crimes against Anita, who was abducted on her way home from the hospital where she worked as a nurse. They totally abused the former beauty queen, leaving her crumpled body in a field, like garbage thrown out a car window. And to add to the horror, it came out in proceedings that they previously practised their depravities on a sheep carcass, taken from the abattoirs where John Travers, one of these sub-human creeps, had worked.

During the lunch break at court one day, I met Garry Lynch and his wife, Peg, and I found it quite impossible to imagine the extent of their pain. Surely, I thought, they must be fantasising about hiring a hit-man to burst into court and shoot the defendants—especially given Mr Lynch had to go on living with the memory of indentifying Anita's battered and defiled body.

> *The root causes of our illnesses and addictions are old hatreds and resentments.*

At sentencing, the judge made clear his contempt: 'There is no doubt that apart from the humiliation, the degradation and terror inflicted upon this young woman, she was the victim of a prolonged and sadistic physical and sexual assault, including repeated sexual assaults anally, orally and vaginally.

'Wild animals are given to pack assaults and killings', he said before a crammed court. 'This is one of the most, if not *the* most, horrifying physical and sexual assaults I have encountered in my forty-odd years associated with the law. The crime is exacerbated by the fact that the victim almost certainly was made aware, in the end, of her pending death.

'Throughout the long trial, the prisoners, albeit, to a lesser degree in the case of the prisoner Murdoch, showed no signs of remorse or contrition. Instead, frequently they were observed to be laughing with one another and were seen sniggering behind their hands.'

All five men was given life imprisonment, with the recommendation the official files of each prisoner should be clearly marked 'never to be released'.

Justice was served, but how on earth do the parents of the victim in a crime such as this manage to go on living without constantly dreaming of punishing those responsible?

Some years later I went out to the Lynch family home, ahead of writing an article honouring Mr Lynch's efforts in setting up an organisation to support the loved ones of homicide victims. He and his wife also talked about a recent trip to India where they embraced eastern religion, which helped stop them from going mad. I suspect this was their salvation, and it allowed them, so Gary Lynch said, to 'forgive the souls' of the animals who killed Anita—although they drew the line at forgiving the men on a mortal, human level.

If forgiving *conditionally* is the best we can do, then sometimes that's enough.

37

HURTING LIKE HELL, BUT FORGIVING ANYWAY

At Garry Lynch's funeral, Ken Marslew was in the packed church to honour his friend. The two men had steadfastly supported each other over many years, since teenager Michael Marslew turned up to his part-time Pizza Hut job, just like other nights—except this didn't play out like other nights. Four young guys arrived to rob the joint and in the bungled robbery, Michael was shot dead, point-blank, in the back of the head with a 12-gauge shotgun.

His dad, Ken, said in an interview some time later, 'Oh, did I think of revenge! I could taste it. I could feel it. I wanted it, I lived it. I spent my whole life at that stage with anger, hate and revenge. That was all I thought about. It's what got me out of bed in the morning. It's what I thought about all day. It's what I went to sleep thinking about of a night-time—getting even.'

And yet somehow he managed to leave that dark place behind, inspiring so many in the process. Not only did he go on to found an anti-violence organisation, but he and Michael's mother agreed to take part in a televised meeting in gaol with several of the culprits, and their parents. It was television the like of which I have never seen before, with heartfelt apologies on one side, and genuine forgiveness on the other.

No longer weighed down by loathing and spite, Ken Marslew was freed up to help others, which he now does, day after day. It's a story with a promising ending, whereas it could so easily have remained all about hopelessness and pain.

Just recently, when Karl Kramer, one of his son's killers, was released after 15 years inside, Ken Marslew was outside the gates to welcome him. He shook hands with the killer, and it was captured by a television crew, invited along to witness the meeting. The subsequent media coverage put Mr Marslew in a very good light for his ability to hold out a hand to the man who had taken Michael's life. I too was swept along by the frenzy built up over this extraordinary, and unlikely, act of solidarity.

I can't, however, ignore a radio interview I heard the next day with Michael's grieving mother, Joan. She was hurting badly at the idea that her ex-husband would be so welcoming to one who had taken part in the execution-style killing of their precious son. She was further outraged that Mr Marslew took a camera crew along to record the moment. I hadn't thought about it until then, but I found myself wondering about the rightness of forgiveness when it punishes innocent people in the process.

From the research I've done about people who've had loved ones senselessly killed or maimed, it's clear that seeing the perpetrators in court, and watching them receive appropriate sentences, can be very soothing. At best it serves as the start of a new beginning. But when the sentence is light or suspended or, worse still, the criminal gets off, then forgiveness is likely to be pushed into the distant future.

I have no idea how they do it, but sometimes grieving parents are interviewed outside court and, irrespective of what kind of sentence was handed down, they say they have no hard feelings. Are these people born extraordinary, or does their greatness come out of their suffering?

The last one to catch my attention was the case of Neil and Fiona Faragher, whose eighteen-year-old son, Andrew, died in a car crash caused by a drunk driver. The driver got three years and four months in gaol—which doesn't seem like much for a life—but outside court the parents said they felt 'neither bitterness nor hatred'.

Mr Faragher told a journalist, 'While he was clearly the cause of Andrew's death, I know he had no intention of harming him in any way. I forgive him for what he has done and I hope he regrets his moment of madness, which will have devastated his family as well as ours. He will have to carry this guilt with him for the rest of his life. It is enough that one life has been destroyed.'

It's clear that seeing perpetrators in court, and watching them receive appropriate sentences, can be soothing.

And the equally remarkable Mrs Faragher added that she felt no anger over the minimum sentence: 'It's not going to change anything. It's not going to bring Andrew back.'

Even more staggering than that is how Marietta Jeager from Montana has made her peace with the man who tortured and raped her seven-year-old daughter, Susie. He then killed and canabalised her. And if you haven't fainted from *those* details, then get this: the deranged low-life phoned Marietta on the first anniversary of Susie's death to taunt her.

Did she swear at him or tell him God had a special place reserved in hell with his name on it? No. She simply asked, 'What can I do to help you?' They then talked for an hour.

She insists her forgiveness was genuine, amazing even her. It seems she had been working on it, and praying, for a year. As she later explained, 'It turned the whole thing around, because his intention was to call and get his kicks and hang up. What undid him was that I asked what I could do to help him. He started crying, and that's when I really realised what a miracle had happened to me. He said, "I wish this burden could be lifted from me", and then he couldn't stop crying. He kept asking me to hang up and I wouldn't because it was my only link to my little girl.'

In talking, the murderer divulged enough information for the authorities to track him down. He later hanged himself in gaol.

Not only did Marietta lose her precious daughter in the most unspeakable of circumstances, but her husband suffered a heart attack and died an early death due to the stress of their loss. This is her take on the longing for retribution: 'Those who maintain a vindictive mindset give the killer another victim. I don't want people to look for reasons not to deal with forgiveness because I know what a gift it is, the healthiness and wholesomeness that it brings to my life.'

She believes that forgiveness is the only way to preserve one's health after a trauma like a child's murder: 'More and more of the medical profession is telling us that the root causes of our illnesses and addictions are old hatreds and resentments. We forgive first of all for our own sake. Spirituality prompted my decision to forgive, but also the knowledge that hatred is not healthy.'

Marietta Jeager went on to co-found Murder Victims' Families for Reconciliation. Also a member is Sue Norton, who forgave Robert Knighton, the man who killed her father and stepmother.

An hour before an Oklahoma jury gave Knighton the death penalty, Sue Norton was sitting outside his cell holding his hand. I found an interview she gave in which she said, 'I came to realise that killing him was not going to take away my hurt.'

While the jury was deliberating, Sue Norton asked for permission to see Knighton. The first thing she told him was she didn't hate him. 'I've never hated anyone in my whole life and I'm not going to start. If you're guilty, I forgive you.'

Then she reached inside the gaol cell and held his hand.

38

JOY AT LAST!

I can't stress enough how much joy is coming my way, now that my antenna is constantly on the lookout for people who are grappling honestly with the issue of forgiveness. Some of them will finally choose reconciliation over retaliation, however great the offence committed against them.

I'm also open to the inspiration, there for the taking, in stories I'm discovering about others who are courageous in alternative ways, and may end up deciding rationally that full-on absolution is not theirs to give.

And how exciting it is to realise that lives we can learn from in this regard are often right in our own backyard, or within our circle, however wide or narrow that might be. We don't need to travel to the other side of the world in order to be blown away by folks under great stress who are behaving with quiet dignity, and being incredibly brave.

One night since starting this project, I was catching up on the phone with a friend and, as we chatted, I suddenly realised that what I was hearing *must* be included in this book. Jacquie Everitt is a fearless human rights lawyer who demonstrated infinite love for a particularly traumatised refugee family and, against the odds, eventually got them justice . . . and almost ten years on, that family has no rage against the system which wronged it, while Jacquie, their advocate, doesn't look like forgiving the transgression. It's an interesting contrast, and it's part of the fall-out from a case which attracted media attention around the world, due to her dogged determination.

I rang Jacquie the next day and asked if I could interview her, and she graciously agreed. She's someone I have on a pedestal because of her first-class brain, her sweetness and her integrity. She doesn't seem to have a clue how extraordinary she is. Just to give you an inkling: she and her husband, Tim, have seven children between them, and when the seventh was a baby, Jacquie went off to university to study law, because her lifelong dream was to become a human rights lawyer. Here is the part of her story that leads up to her wrestling with forgiveness . . . told over ginger tea and banana bread in my living room.

Jacquie had just come back from East Timor, where she'd been working as deputy director of a humanitarian aid agency after the referendum for East Timor to separate from Indonesia. There was such violence—mass murder, rapes, burnings and killings—and having seen such horrors in those refugee camps, as well as Vietnamese refugees in camps in Malaysia, the images never went out of her head:

> We'd been running clinics in East Timor, and everyone was traumatised; it's a kind of frozenness, and you see it. They're totally passive and they don't want to talk. They don't want to answer your questions, and the first man I interviewed

was just like that . . . and the raped women were exactly like this too . . . there was a lot of rape by the Indonesians in East Timor. There were a lot of rape babies, and you'd have a woman holding a rape baby and they had what the doctors called PE . . . pain everywhere . . . it's trauma.

She returned home because both her parents were dying.

'When they died, it made me value the preciousness of life, and I realised it must be dedicated to not only living your own life well, but helping other people. I know that sounds absolutely pathetic and I feel embarrassed saying it, but that was the effect the death of my parents had on me, to reinforce the sanctity of life.'

By now Jacquie had a law degree she hadn't yet done anything with, and once the funerals were over she volunteered to work in a community legal service. Soon she was given a permanent job, which took her into a refugee detention camp.

'On my first visit I saw the same trauma on the faces of the people there as I had witnessed in the disgusting camps in East Timor, and this place was just as bad. I was absolutely transfixed and I said to the other lawyer with me, who was teaching me how to be a refugee lawyer, "These people are traumatised", and she said, "Oh are they?" and I was amazed she didn't recognise it.'

Jacquie couldn't believe there were children locked up, surrounded by guards:

By the time I got back to the office I thought, this is outrageous; then a few weeks later I saw a compelling piece in the paper about a Dr Aamer Sultan, an inmate at the camp who was a doctor from Iraq. So I immediately rang and asked to come and see him. This man is just fascinating—especially about forgiveness, because he's forgiven everybody.

He's incredibly bright, and I talked to him about the children, and he sighed, 'Ah, the children. That's the worst thing. Actually I'm doing research on the children and writing a paper on it.'

I asked to meet some of them, because I myself was doing a Masters in International Law and I explained I'd like to do a thesis on this, and he said, 'You want to meet kids do you? Well you're not going to believe this: there's a child in here who's catatonic.'

So this is how Jacquie first met the Bedraie family from Iran. This child, Shayan, had been in hospital five or six times by this stage to be rehydrated because he was refusing to eat; he was only six and had been in detention for about eighteen months. Jacquie was frank with me about the fact that the family's refugee status was completely irrelevant to her.

'I didn't even want to know people's stories; I didn't want to get involved with them—it started out as forensic research on my part.'

That detachment went out the window as soon as she saw Shayan. 'I knew he was dying', she explained.

I looked at him and it was like an arrow that came up through my feet and went right through me, this icy arrow—and I stood there dumbfounded. I couldn't speak. He was like a puppet hanging down over his father's shoulder, and I went round the back of him and his head was hanging down, and I took his hands in my hands and they were like ice.

It was a freezing, wet day and there was mud everywhere. It was revolting, and the rain was pelting down on the tin roof of the shelter where you visit people. I said, 'Hello, Shayan. I was so looking forward to meeting you.' No response, and so I moved my hand back and forth in front of his face; no reaction, and all I wanted to do was cry.

The parents were very, very, very passive and compliant; they didn't seem to know what was going on at all. They told me the things they had seen and the things that had happened to them; then they just wanted to get away from me, because talking to me had made them confront the horrors of what they had been through.

I thought, why don't they scream? Why don't they thump these guards in the chest and say, 'For Christ's sake get me a doctor', but then I realised they had done all that, and nothing's happened.

When they were leaving the shelter I was crying, and I felt so ashamed and disgusted that this could happen. I was a woman of privilege, I'd had an education, and I know how to do things; this could never happen to my child; it couldn't— but it happened to *this* child, because this child was a boat person.

Was he not as valuable as my child? Because his parents were perceived to have done something wrong by not having the right papers—does that matter? He's an innocent child.

Jacquie made the decision that she couldn't turn her back on this boy and his family—even though she didn't imagine she could do anything, because she didn't think she had much legal expertise. Plus she was all too aware that the family had been rejected on their application for refugee status:

But to my mind it didn't actually matter . . . this child had got sick here, and I assumed that was linked to the trauma of having seen a man slash his wrists in detention and the blood spurt out. He believed the man had died, even though that wasn't the case, and that's when he became catatonic. He stopped eating, and his parents didn't know what to do.

As I left, I said to them, 'I promise you'll get out of here', but I had no idea how I was going to do this. Meanwhile, of course, the child had to be made well.

Right around the planet at any one time there are millions of displaced people suffering greatly. Jacquie knew that, but it was the Bedraies with whom she was now up close and personal. She just couldn't walk away.

Being a journalist as well as a lawyer, Jacquie began a campaign that included going public with chilling drawings by Shayan, and publishing pictures she had taken with a camera she sneaked into the camp. Soon the world's media was paying attention:

The drawings were almost identical to those I'd seen in the Holocaust Museum . . . the clothing is different, but you could think you were looking at the same thing, and I had a really chilling photo of the man, just after he'd slashed his wrists.

As well, the mother had given me other drawings by Shayan of his family in which the two children have got tears falling and there's razor wire everywhere and a guard holding a baton—and these batons were used during the camp riots witnessed by Shayan. The guard in the drawing is yelling into a radio, and also in the picture is a caged van which was used to take him to hospital.

He became more and more sick; he became seriously sick, and nine times he was taken to hospital for rehydration, and never once was he assessed in hospital. Look, the whole refugee issue is a very shaming thing for anyone who's experienced it, and what fascinated me is that people worked in this place and they didn't scream out, they didn't go to the media. They got paid well. Actually, I can forgive more the prison guards who worked there more than I can forgive the public servants.

After that bleak, rainy day in the camp when Jacquie first met Shayan and his family, she became determined to make a difference, and soon his horrible story was seen on network television.

'This child had now escaped into living rooms. He had been seen—and he couldn't be unseen', Jacquie recalled.

> *Will I ever forgive? No, and I don't think*
> *I should.*

'By now I was getting very angry. I had expected, as a response to my story, an outcry from child psychiatrists, nurses, teachers, doctors—all the people who care for children to say, "Stop it. There will be no more"—but this didn't happen.'

Shayan was put into foster care, becoming even more traumatised. The destruction of a child was being played out, and Jacquie was way past treating this case forensically:

This family had become *my* family.

When you become an advocate it becomes an obsessive thing—and it's at the expense of other things in your life, and it was definitely at the expense of my own children. My husband was very good and he picked up the reins, and he has always been a very involved father; but the fact remains that I neglected my own children to look after someone else's child . . . but that child was in great peril . . . so it became a complete crusade. I was utterly fearless . . . but then I'm a middle-class well-educated woman—what could they do to me? I live a privileged life.

In the end the family's claim to be granted refugee status was reassessed, and the previous decision overturned. The Bedraies were found to be genuine asylum seekers.

Once the family had refugee status, it took me a while, but I wanted them to take the case to court, claiming compensation for the damage done to Shayan—because that's what a civilised society does: if someone is damaged, you can't give a child back his childhood, but you can compensate by giving him money to provide security for the future.

It took me a long time to convince them to go ahead, but in the end we went to court. They [the authorities] fought us all the way and settled out of court. It took eight months.

Shayan is now 13 and is a student at an exceptional high school. He was under enormous stress during his formative years between five and seven, which set him back, and he has a lot of catching up to do. I've observed him at a party Jacquie gave and I can say that he looks great, a typical teenager in baseball cap and sneakers. Life is good for the family now. They have a house which belongs to Shayan and they feel very safe. They love their home.

Jacquie is no longer angry, but has she forgiven?

'No, I haven't forgiven. I haven't forgiven the bureaucrats. I know every one of their names because I've seen all the court documents. *How* could they have allowed this to happen? How?'

I asked Jacquie Everitt if she would prefer it if she *could* forgive in this situation?

I think there's an element of wanting to maintain the rage—because it can happen again.

I've met holocaust survivors who attend the little synagogue in the street where I used to live. I'd chat to the old men as they walked past, and discovered that every one of them has forgiven. I've never met one who hasn't . . . but I've encountered *children* of holocaust survivors who haven't forgiven, and never will. And I think I'm like that: it's partly to do with the need for eternal vigilance, but it's also because there are people who haven't been brought to justice.

It doesn't matter if these people are eighty-six, they have to be brought to justice, because it's not acceptable for the millions to do the bidding of the bosses either when it's wrong. You cannot just say, 'We were just doing our job'. The Nuremberg defence just doesn't wash.

The Bedraies aren't filled with rage. They have forgiven, and Jacquie figures they were never enraged the way she was. They'd taken a gamble on a new life and were smuggled out of their country. They were accepting of being locked up, knowing they had a refugee claim, knowing it was going to happen, and when it didn't happen they were bewildered. They couldn't understand it.

'They're very controlled, very passive people and they have let it go. Yes, they have forgiven.'

Is clinging to this resentment holding Jacquie back in life generally?

It's taken nearly eight years of my life, and I've had to go through all the stages you go through with a death, but the Bedraies didn't appear to go through all that, I guess because their expectations are so different to mine.

Will I ever forgive? No, and I don't think I should. I don't mean to be self-righteous about this—and there's definitely an element of self-indulgence in wallowing in anger—but I honestly don't believe I should forgive, just as I don't think the children of the holocaust survivors should forgive the Nazis. Same thing with the children of victims of the Pol Pot regime in Cambodia; I know many, many victims of Pol Pot, and they just want to get on with their lives—but now I think the younger generation there feels differently.

In my case, maybe because it wasn't done to me personally, I can indulge myself. I think your brain knows what you can do and what you can't do and my brain is letting me still be filled with angst, and I can afford that luxury . . . but like the holocaust survivors, the Bedraies had to let go in order to survive. It's about survival.

I was thrilled to attend the launch of *The Bitter Shore*, the book Jacquie wrote about this case. The Badraie family was warmly applauded as they arrived at the party, and Zahra, Shayan's mother, asked if she could address the guests. Clearly way out of her comfort zone, she was determined to publically thank Jacquie for making their dream come true.

THE FORGIVENESS DIET

The coolest bad boy on the planet is P. Diddy. Right? He could read the telephone book out loud and women everywhere would sigh with delight.

Back in 2007, P. Diddy launched his perfume called Unforgiveable Woman. It's a catchy name, but what the hell does it mean? I turned to an interview of the rapper by India-Jewell Jackson, Beauty Editor of the Glam Blush website. As any sane person would, she asked P. Diddy what gives with the name Unforgiveable. He told her:

> Unforgivable is a positive thing—it's really about your belief in yourself. Being unapologetic and having that confidence in yourself; being a leader. If you're not apologizing, then people can't forgive you. If you believe in who you are, even if you're different, that makes you 'unforgivable.' It's your swagger. It's your confidence. It's your attitude.

That comment fits in perfectly with his highly-marketable 'screw you' public persona—but I can't say I like him encouraging others to trample the rest of the population in a Sherman tank, never apologising for the damage done.

Mind you, I'm probably being churlish because I didn't think of the perfume idea first—although of course mine would have been called 'Forgive'.

This morning I came up with an even better idea: *The Forgiveness Diet*. So far it's only a concept, but I see it as a sure-fire way to draw attention to this topic I have become so passionate about. Diets, however stupid, manage to get coverage in most mainstream magazines and on lifestyle TV programs, so why not *The Forgiveness Diet*? It's no sillier than the popular Flat Belly Diet or the South Beach Diet, and when I'm interviewed about it I could segue from dieting . . . to the importance of forgiveness for those who are going nowhere in life because they're stuck in an emotional war zone.

Oh dear, bad idea, because I just remembered I can't cook. Lives might be lost if unsuspecting readers followed my culinary suggestions.

You know something else I have against diets? I have a strong belief that those of us who are plumper than we'd like to be need to stop being so hard on ourselves, and turn our backs on the culture of permanent dieting. I'm talking *self*-forgiveness as regards weight, and I'm smiling here as I recall a friend of mine, Marita, who was complaining that her jeans were tight because she'd eaten too much pasta on a holiday to Italy. She was beating up on herself over the weight gain and the difficulty she was having squeezing into her Levis when a gay guy we know cut in with the perfect solution: 'So go up a size.'

Hearing that comment really created a shift in my lifelong tendency towards crying whenever I see the unwelcome results on my hips of a serious pig-out. Just go up a size.

Being hard on ourselves with regard to weight gain is the perfect example of the kind of self-loathing that could easily end up defining us. And if we despise *ourselves*, feeling constantly guilty about how we look or about some mistake we've made, surely we're much less likely to give others a break, or give them the benefit of the doubt. From my own experience, life can then become predominantly about clinging to the wreckage of unresolved issues.

And here's another arena in which we often wallow in guilt: when our actions or desires go against what was rammed into us by the faith in which we were brought up. I was raised a Catholic, so I'm an expert, while various Jewish pals of mine have always joked about how Jewish guilt never goes away either. Shouldn't we, though, give ourselves permission to lead happy lives without any guilt or shame? And if we're less tough on *ourselves*, aren't we more likely to seek resolution with others we've been feeling vindictive towards?

Speaking of religion, it's tempting, is it not, for us to play God and decide that he or she who has sinned against us doesn't deserve to be forgiven? And the bookend to that is if we decide God Himself doesn't deserve to be forgiven when great tragedy strikes.

It takes a mighty leap of faith to get past deep hurt and disaster, especially when the victims (either ourselves, or others we care about) are innocent of wrongdoing. God would say to turn the other cheek, but that can be very hard indeed. Maybe all we can do is trust that fate has a sweet consolation for us, just around the corner—especially if we can first find a way to relinquish the longing to square up.

I'm not a psychiatrist, and I don't even have a PhD. My only qualification in all of this is that I've made a million mistakes, and repaired a few of them. I know how good it feels to hold out a hand of friendship after years of anger; plus my research for this book has taught me a great deal too.

And if we're less tough on ourselves, aren't we more likely to seek resolution with others we've been feeling vindictive towards?

After speaking to all these fine people, as well as reflecting on my own experiences, I'm beginning to suspect that there is a tangible shift that happens in the brain when we stop being so tough on ourselves and others, and go for peace. If I'm wrong—so shoot me—but if I'm right, then how fabulous is that!

I'll tell you something else I've discovered on this adventure: relationships forged in the context of a shared enthusiasm for the power of forgiveness tend to be incredibly positive and supportive, while conversely, of course, friendships based on a mutual passion for say alcohol, drugs or crime are more likely to have a Kamikaze dynamic.

Adrianna Scheibner, for example, has gone from being someone I once interviewed to a person I really look forward to seeing. When we catch up, the conversation is largely about the negativity each of us has left behind, and the good times that are already here.

Having a caring support network like this results in us all passing around books that reinforce life-affirming beliefs—and these gestures are precious presents, because just one line written by a wise person can help us to soar, and to bring about true healing.

The latest book Adrianna has lent me is *Transcending The Levels of Consciousness* by David R. Hawkins, MD PhD. Sorry Doc, but so far your concepts are proving a bit too grown-up for me. However, I have found one glittering prize in there that I fully get, and I hope you won't mind if I include it here, because it's quite wonderful:

> *When one willingly lets a hated perpetrator 'off the hook' by forgiveness, it is not that person who is taken off the hook, but oneself.*

I like it in self-help books when they have a page at the end of each chapter summing up the life-altering key points within that section. Unfortunately in *my* case, I couldn't come up with enough pearls of wisdom for a summation after each chapter. Apologies for that, but I'm still on my trainer wheels as an amateur life coach. I'm definitely no Oscar Wilde, legendary for tossing off unforgettable one-liners with little effort, such as, 'Always forgive your enemies—nothing infuriates them so!' Shit, why didn't *I* come up with that one?

All I now know for absolute certain about forgiveness can be reduced to the following top-ten tips . . .

1. Human beings are hard-wired for bliss. (Thank you for that Candace Pert.)
2. Revenge is not all it's cracked up to be.
3. If you can't remember why you hate someone, it's definitely time to give them a 'get out of gaol' card.

4. Without doubt, one of the hardest things in the world to cope with is when the person next to you in a Pilates class does that really annoying yoga breathing. It's way too loud and was especially driving me around the bend this morning, because there's a new guy in our class who's guilty of this and by chance he always seems to park himself near me. Seriously, would it kill him to move up the back near the two women who never stop talking? I was so close to squirting him with my water bottle today . . . but then I remembered I no longer hold grudges. I managed a few deep breaths of my own, sent a silent blessing to the brother alongside me, and calm was immediately restored to our corner of the studio as I focused on the fact that he had done nothing wrong. And if a late-bloomer like me can rise above the tendency to blame everyone but herself—then it should be a breeze for you.

5. If you loathe someone for what you *believe* they said or did—chances are they have a completely different take on what happened. Who's right? Maybe *they* are—or perhaps neither version is on the money. Forgiveness looks like a real smart option when you might be wrong anyway.

6. Remaining riddled with spite, and hating with passion, will take its toll and give you wrinkles. And it means you'll have much less energy for the good things in life, such as loving, laughing and happy endings.

7. Thin-skinned people are more likely to see red and hold a grudge—so the trick is to unlearn that behaviour. Act as if you're thick-skinned, and hopefully you'll soon have the hang of it.

8. Live in the moment. That's all there is—and no amount of wishing will erase the day you wounded a friend, or *they*

caused *you* heartache. It happened, and today it's ancient history. *Now* is the time to be happy, and the bonus is that when you forgive, it's *you* who gets the gift.

9. Forgive *everyone* (if you can) . . . and if the door is sometimes slammed in your face when you turn up with an olive branch, what do you care? You'll *still* feel better than you did when you were carrying round all that rage.

10. Don't wait too long.

PS: I know I said I had ten tips, but I just remembered another one, and it's important. Here it is: beautiful people are forgiven their wicked deeds much more readily than the rest of us are. We all get that, but I just want to say it's not their fault they have a seemingly easier ride through life—so maybe we should give them a break. Eventually.